INTERNATIONAL TRADE IN SERVICES: BANKING

IDENTIFICATION AND ANALYSIS OF OBSTACLES

ORGANISATION FOR ECONOMIC CO-OPERATION AND DEVELOPMENT

Pursuant to article 1 of the Convention signed in Paris on 14th December, 1960, and which came into force on 30th September, 1961, the Organisation for Economic Co-operation and Development (OECD) shall promote policies designed:

- to achieve the highest sustainable economic growth and employment and a rising standard of living in Member countries, while maintaining financial stability, and thus to contribute to the development of the world economy;
- to contribute to sound economic expansion in Member as well as non-member countries in the process of economic development; and
- to contribute to the expansion of world trade on a multilateral, non-discriminatory basis in accordance with international obligations.

The Signatories of the Convention on the OECD are Austria, Belgium, Canada, Denmark, France, the Federal Republic of Germany, Greece, Iceland, Ireland, Italy, Luxembourg, the Netherlands, Norway, Portugal, Spain, Sweden, Switzerland, Turkey, the United Kingdom and the United States. The following countries acceded subsequently to this Convention (the dates are those on which the instruments of accession were deposited): Japan (28th April, 1964), Finland (28th January, 1969), Australia (7th June, 1971) and New Zealand (29th May, 1973).

The Socialist Federal Republic of Yugoslavia takes part in certain work of the OECD (agreement of 28th October, 1961).

Publié en français sous le titre :

ÉCHANGES INTERNATIONAUX
DE SERVICE: SECTEUR BANCAIRE
RECENSEMENT ET ANALYSE
DES OBSTACLES

Since the Second World War great progress has been achieved in the liberalisation of international trade in both goods and services. In the OECD, Member countries' undertakings to eliminate restrictions among themselves in current invisible operations and transfers have been recorded in the Code of Liberalisation of Current Invisible Operations. A substantial number of restrictions to trade in services still exist, nevertheless, and the OECD Council, aware of the increasing importance of the service sector in the economy of most Member countries requested the Committees of the Organisation responsible for these sectors to study and assess the obstacles to trade in services in order to find ways to remove unjustified impediments and improve international co-operation in this area. The Council instructed the Committee on Financial Markets to survey impediments to international trade in banking services.

In defining the scope of the enquiry, the Committee did not formulate a rigorous definition of banking services, but accepted the definition of banking that exists in each Member country. A detailed questionnaire was sent to Member countries enquiring about restrictive practices in banking and related activities. Simultaneously, the Business and Industry Advisory Committee, BIAC, was consulted in order to determine whether private banks operating outside their countries of domicile believed that they were being subjected to discriminatory treatment. Based upon these enquiries, the study discusses restrictive practices in the following four general areas, regardless of whether the restrictive practice arises from explicit legislation or from administrative practice:

A. De-novo Entry and Establishment of Foreign Banking Organisations;

B. Acquisition by Foreign Banking Organisations of Participations in Indigenous Banks;

C. Operations of Established Foreign-Owned Banking Organisations;

D. Cross-Border International Banking Operations.

The report discusses in general terms how restrictive practices in each category of operation are formulated and then specifies the restrictive practices that exist in each Member country. Within each category of operation, the study outlines the full range of restrictions that Member countries apply. Thus, in discussing equity participation by foreign institutions, attention is given to related issues, such as rules governing foreign branches and/or subsidiaries, and requirements of reciprocity. In discussing the issue of National Treatment, issues considered include differential capital requirements and operations which are explicitly prohibited to foreign-based institutions. Discussion of restrictions on cross-border operations includes both controls on lending and on deposit taking or solicitation.

The present volume represents the conclusion of the first step in the ongoing effort of the OECD to promote liberalisation in trade in banking services. While more work remains to be done in this domain, it is believed that the publication of an internationally agreed list of restrictions furthers the process of liberalisation by highlighting issues on which future liberalisation effort will have to focus and by making the full extent of restrictive practices known to interested parties inside and outside OECD Member governments.

Also available

"Trends in Banking Structure and Regulation in OECD Countries":

THE INTERNATIONALISATION OF BANKING – The Policy Issues by R.M. Pecchioli (November 1983)
(21 83 04 1) ISBN 92-64-12488-8 222 pages   £11.00   US$22.00   F110.00

BANKING AND ELECTRONIC FUND TRANSFERS by Professor J.R.S. Revell (November 1983)
(21 83 05 1) ISBN 92-64-12505-1 202 pages   £11.00   US$22.00   F110.00

***

INTERNATIONAL TRADE IN SERVICES: INSURANCE. Identification and Analysis of Obstacles (February 1984)
(21 84 01 1) ISBN 92-64-12552-3 78 pages   £5.00   US$10.00   F50.00

Prices charged at the OECD Publications Office.

*THE OECD CATALOGUE OF PUBLICATIONS and supplements will be sent free of charge
on request addressed either to OECD Publications Office,
2, rue André-Pascal, 75775 PARIS CEDEX 16, or to the OECD Sales Agent in your country.*

LIST OF CONTENTS

6

INTRODUCTION

At its March 1982 meeting, the Committee on Financial Markets agreed to undertake a Member country survey of obstacles to trade in services in the banking sector which would serve as a basis for an analysis of the nature and significance of the identified obstacles in keeping with the Committee's mandate to contribute to the Organisation's trade in services exercise.

In determining the scope of the survey, the Committee agreed to adopt a broad definition of "trade in services", encompassing (i) "establishment trade in services", which involves the establishment of the foreign-controlled bank supplying banking services in the country of the consumer of those services; (ii) "across-the-border trade in services", which relates to those banking services which are provided by a bank in the exporting country to a consumer of those services in another country; and (iii) trade-in-service operations arising from a combination of these two approaches (e.g. the establishment of foreign-controlled banks in a financial centre to participate in the provision of banking services to customers in third countries). Accordingly, the enquiry was extended to cover the following areas:

A. De-Novo Entry and Establishment of Foreign Banking Organisations.

B. Acquisition by Foreign Banking Organisations of Participations in Indigenous Banks.

C. Operations of Established Foreign-Owned Banking Organisations.

D. Cross-Border International Banking Operations.

With a view to properly identifying the impediments existing in the banking sector, Member countries were invited to reply to a "Questionnaire on Possible Obstacles to International Banking Operations" (Annex I). The results of this survey, together with comments submitted by the Capital Movements and Capital Markets Committee of the Business and Industry Advisory Committee (BIAC), were discussed by the Committee on Financial Markets which agreed on the text of the inventory of impediments to international banking operations which is annexed to this report (Annex II).

The second task undertaken by the Committee was to survey existing obstacles arising from legal provisions or administrative practices which discriminate against foreign banks which bear more heavily on foreign banks. The Committee carried out an assessment of the relative importance of such obstacles, focusing on the extent to which they may be regarded as "substantial" in the sense that either they prevent, or definitely discourage, international banking operations and investment in the banking sector by non-resident banks, or result in discrimination against banks under foreign control. The results of the Committee's analysis are presented in Section I below.

The analysis of the results of the survey has brought out the relevance of existing OECD investment instruments (1) with regard to the four broad areas in which restraints on trade in banking services may arise through either official restrictions or discriminatory administrative practices. Section II of the present report examines the relationships between OECD instruments and impediments to international banking operations.

Section I

ANALYSIS AND ASSESSMENT OF OBSTACLES TO
INTERNATIONAL BANKING OPERATIONS

SOME GENERAL CONSIDERATIONS

When trying to identify obstacles to trade in banking services, a major problem relates to the difficulty of properly defining what constitutes an obstacle. The conditions under which a banking organisation can conduct business in a foreign country or with residents of a foreign country are determined by a host of elements ranging from legislative and regulatory provisions, related inter alia to prudential surveillance and to the conduct of monetary and credit policy, through administrative practices to purely market-related factors, such as the existence of private restrictive practices and the degree of competition in the financial services industry. Although the Committee's exercise focuses on existing restraints arising from government regulations, policies and administrative practices, an assessment of the relative importance of such impediments cannot disregard the influence of other factors which may affect foreign banking business in a given country.

For the purpose of the present exercise, the analysis concerns impediments resulting from (i) the existence of provisions which discriminate against services provided by non-resident foreign banking organisations, including discriminatory restrictions on right of establishment; (ii) an exception to National Treatment with regard to the operations of foreign-controlled banks established in the country under consideration; and (iii) administrative practices that bear more heavily on foreign banking organisations.

The present analysis does not address a certain number of instances where regulatory provisions and requirements which are applied uniformly to both domestic and foreign-controlled banks in practice fall with particular severity on the latter. In order not to delay the preparation of this report, the Committee considered that any specific problems of this nature due to regulations which do not intentionally discriminate against foreign-owned banks but which, nevertheless, limit their competitive opportunities should be dealt with at a later stage. Similarly, the Committee decided to address the general issue of transparency of regulations and administrative practices applying to international banking operations only after completion of the present phase of the exercise.

It should be noted that the information collected from countries, and which forms the basis for the analysis presented in this report, uses the national definitions of "banks" and "banking services". It would have been very time consuming to seek to achieve homogeneity in the coverage of impediments to be analysed through a standardisation of the definition of banking services. It does not appear that the conclusions of the analysis are substantially affected by certain divergencies that have been noted between national practices depending on the extent to which individual countries adopt a narrower or a broader definition of "banks". The Committee intends, however, to address this question at a later stage in its work together with the more important question of how to accommodate in the analysis the notable increase experienced in recent years in many countries of the number of financial institutions conducting some, or all, of the market activities previously carried out solely by "banks" in the traditional meaning of the term.

The Committee has identified four areas in which restraints on trade in banking services may arise through either official restrictions or discriminatory administrative practices:

    A. De-Novo Entry and Establishment of Foreign Banking Organisations;

    B. Acquisition by Foreign Banking Organisations of Participations in Indigenous Banks;

    C. Operations of Established Foreign-Controlled Banking Organisations;

    D. Cross-Border International Banking Operations.

The remainder of the present section sets out an assessment of existing impediments to international banking operations in each of these four areas.

A. DE-NOVO ENTRY AND ESTABLISHMENT OF FOREIGN BANKING ORGANISATIONS

The position of individual Member countries with regard to the entry and establishment de-novo of foreign banking organisations is summarised in Tables 1.1 to 1.3 of Annex II, covering respectively:

    Table 1.1.   Regulatory provisions governing the entry and establishment of foreign banks

    Table 1.2.   Reciprocity provisions concerning the establishment of foreign banking organisations

    Table 1.3.   Other requirements, restrictions and impediments affecting foreign bank entry.

Without attempting to analyse or evaluate in detail at this stage the different rationales that exist for imposing restrictions on the entry of foreign banks, it appears that these vary considerably from country to country. The attitudes of each country flow from historical factors, from the degree of sophistication and development of the domestic market and from general attitudes towards the value of, and need for, competition in the financial services industry. Just where a country strikes the balance of costs and benefits of an open-door policy in the banking sector is not fixed once and for all and, indeed, in recent years there have been some quite significant shifts in attitudes (2). Prohibition of, or the placing of strict limits on, foreign bank entry usually stems from the feeling that banking is somehow different from industrial or commercial activities insofar as banking plays a special role in the attainment of national policy goals as a strategic sector for the proper functioning of the economy and one which performs a number of functions of a semi-public nature.

At a less elevated level of generality, a foreign banking presence affects the competitive balance in a national financial system and changes in the latter may not be thought to be desirable. Indigenous banks may be seen as not being sufficiently equipped to withstand competition from more sophisticated foreign institutions. The arrival of foreign banks can also be seen as leading to "overbanking" or to such banks appropriating to themselves the most profitable types of business. Thus, entry restrictions may be modulated to extract the maximum benefit to be derived from a degree of foreign banking presence, but still keeping control over the number and size of foreign institutions allowed to enter the domestic market. Gaining reciprocal access for domestic banks abroad has been a powerful factor opening up access for foreign banks in a number of OECD countries in recent years.

A very general concern with regard to foreign bank entry stems from possible circumvention, or dilution, of domestic monetary policy and prudential controls. Arrangements to confine entry to foreign banks with well-established reputation and to ensure that those admitted into the domestic market are subjected to adequate monetary and supervisory control are quite common and desirable.

With regard to foreign bank establishment, restrictions may concern licensing, reciprocity requirements, and other operational terms on which the licence is granted. The precise form of restraints and administrative practices differs significantly from country to country according to the specific organisational forms under which foreign banks may establish a presence.

Licensing

In the field of foreign bank entry, the question of the right of establishment is uppermost under current licensing rules, or similar authorisations. The following paragraphs summarise the present situation with regard to licensing in Member countries of representative offices, branches and agencies, and subsidiaries of foreign banks. The distinction between these various organisational forms is a fundamental one in terms of legal and regulatory provisions (3).

i) Representative Offices

No Member country prohibits the establishment of representative offices by foreign banking organisations. Indeed, no prior authorisation is required in a number of countries -- i.e. Austria, Denmark, France, Germany, Italy,

Netherlands, New Zealand, Norway, the United Kingdom and the United States -- although in some cases the authorities must be notified. In the other countries, requests by foreign banks to establish representative offices are liberally treated provided that some specific conditions are met (in particular that the representative office does not directly engage in banking business) and that certain documentation is supplied to the authorising body. The submission by the BIAC Committee on Capital Movements and Capital Markets does not contain any indication of complaints by banks with regard to the treatment of foreign banks' applications for the opening of representative offices in Member countries.

ii) Agencies and Branches

The entry and establishment of foreign banks' agencies and branches is prohibited by law or not permitted under current policy in seven Member countries, i.e. Australia, Canada, Finland, Iceland, New Zealand, Norway, and Sweden. In all these countries except Canada, Finland and Norway, the prohibition of foreign branch entry is part and parcel of the general policy not to grant authority to foreign interests to carry on banking business through off-shoots located in the country. The Canadian authorities have explicitly stated that they wish foreign banks to operate in Canada through locally-incorporated entities, rather than branches or agencies, so as to subject them strictly to Canadian law and to facilitate their oversight by the supervisory agencies. In Finland, too, foreign banks can enter the domestic market via subsidiaries but not through branches for the same reasons as in Canada. In addition, the legal existence of foreign branches as an organisational form in banking is not recognised by Finnish legislation. In Portugal the entry and establishment of foreign banks' agencies and branches was prohibited in 1977. However, this prohibition was removed by Decree Law No. 406 of 19 November 1983.

All other Member countries authorise the licensing of foreign banks' branches, subject to a number of specific requirements to be complied with by the applicant. A special case is that of the United States where the establishment of an agency or a branch requires either a federal licence granted by the Comptroller of the Currency or a state licence. Some states expressly prohibit the establishment of agencies and branches of foreign banks (4).

iii) Subsidiaries

Foreign bank entry through subsidiaries is prohibited by law or not permitted under current policy in Australia, Iceland, New Zealand, and Sweden. In Australia, the Government is considering the recommendations of a report by a small group (the Martin Group) concerning the structure of the financial system, including the question of foreign bank entry. Government policy with regard to entry of foreign banks' subsidiaries is presently under review in Sweden. In Norway, the Parliament recently approved changes in policy which will allow foreign bank entry through subsidiaries. The Government intends to follow a step-by-step strategy by initially allowing only a limited number of foreign bank subsidiaries. It is not yet clear when the change is going to take effect. In Canada, foreign banks are permitted to establish subsidiaries in the form of locally-incorporated Schedule B banks, viz. closely-held banks. The possibility of entry is limited indirectly by a regulation which stipulates that the overall volume of domestic assets of federally-incorporated foreign bank subsidiaries may not exceed 8 per cent of total domestic assets of all banks. The ceiling is enforced through control over deemed authorised capital, with a limitation that a subsidiary's total domestic assets may not exceed twenty times its deemed authorised capital. This provision constitutes a specific constraint on foreign bank subsidiaries' capacity to expand business in Canada (5). In Portugal, foreign bank entry through subsidiaries was prohibited by law in 1977 but foreign participation was permitted in parabanking institutions (e.g. investment and leasing companies) and in regional development companies. However, the above-mentioned prohibition was eliminated by the Decree Law No. 406 of 19 November 1983.

All other countries permit the establishment of subsidiaries on the basis of the licensing procedures governing the entry of new banks into the domestic market. In some instances, special procedures are applied for granting the authorisation (6). More generally, a number of countries apply reciprocity tests and specific rerquirements which must be satisfied in order to obtain a licence.

Reciprocity

The present situation concerning the application of reciprocity provisions to foreign bank entry is summarised in Table I. In eleven Member countries, reciprocity tests are, or may be, applied when considering foreign banks' application for entry. The reciprocity principle is embodied in national banking legislation in a number of countries (Canada, Italy, Japan, Spain, Switzerland) and administrative practices take account of reciprocity considerations to a varying extent in Denmark, Finland, France, Ireland and Turkey. Within the EEC, credit institutions having their head office in a Member state are granted a right of entry and establishment following the First Council Directive of December 1977 on the "co-ordination of laws, regulations and administrative provisions relating to the taking up and pursuit of the business of credit institutions". This Directive provides, however, for the principle of reciprocity being applied with regard to branches of credit institutions having their head offices outside the European Community.

In the banking field, the application of reciprocity provisions by Member countries appears to be exercised with considerable flexibility, within the scope of existing legal provisions. Thus, no country applies reciprocity in its strictest formulation whereby a country would authorise the establishment of a foreign bank office only on condition that the home country of the applicant authorises a similar office, on a one-for-one basis, to operate on its domestic market. Generally, host countries which give weight to reciprocity require that the applicant's home country permits some form of foreign bank entry, not necessarily identical to the one sought for by the applicant. Given the wide institutional differences existing across countries, it is recognised that the application of strict reciprocity tests would be difficult in practical terms. Hence, countries usually follow a case-by-case approach, with reciprocity being one of the various requirements (and not necessarily the most important one) to be satisfied for the granting of the necessary entry authorisations.

Table I

RECIPROCITY PROVISIONS

Reciprocity tests apply with regard to foreign bank entry	Yes	No	Not applicable (1)
Australia			X
Austria		X	
Belgium		X	
Canada	X		
Denmark	X(2)		
Finland	X		
France	X(2)		
Germany		X	
Greece		X	
Iceland			X
Ireland	X(2)		
Italy	X(2)		
Japan	X		
Luxembourg		X	
Netherlands	X(2)(3)		
New Zealand			X
Norway			
Portugal			
Spain	X		
Sweden			X
Switzerland	X		
Turkey	X		
United Kingdom		X	
United States			X(4)

1. Foreign bank entry not permitted.

2. Applies only to banks from non-EEC countries.

3. The directives necessary for the application of reciprocity tests have not been issued.

4. Some states apply reciprocity provisions with regard to the entry of foreign banks' agencies and branches.

14

Reciprocity provisions may be used as an instrument for limiting foreign access to the domestic banking system. In practice, to attain such an objective, a rigid application of the reciprocity principle is required -- which is not the case in Member countries. By and large, the primary reason for having recourse to a reciprocity-based policy by a number of countries pursuing a comparatively liberal approach towards foreign bank entry is to use it as a means for gaining facilities of establishment in other countries. The internationalisation of banking, and the need for all countries to ensure that their domestic banks can participate in international business, has meant that, in most instances, considerations of reciprocity have had the effect in practice of opening up more domestic markets to foreign banks.

Other Requirements

Apart from the possibility of obtaining a licence or an equivalent authorisation for establishment, foreign bank entry in a national banking system is affected by the specific requirements attached to the granting of the licence or authorisation. By and large, it would appear that countries permitting foreign bank entry apply the same criteria and requirements as for entry of domestic banks. In a number of areas, however, banks are subject to differential treatment which, though not necessarily intended to discriminate against foreign banks, may bear more heavily on the latter.

A special problem concerns the setting of minimum capital endowment levels and the definition of own funds for branches of foreign banks which, because of their legal nature, cannot be assimilated fully to locally-incorporated banks. In most countries, the minimum earmarked capital of a foreign branch has been set at the same level as the minimum capital required for new domestic banks, though the definition of the branch's own capital takes in some cases explicit account of the branch's net positon vis-à-vis its parent institution. A number of exceptions seem, however, worth mentioning. In Italy and Turkey the amount of the minimum capital endowment for new foreign branches is set by the authority irrespective of the requirement applied to domestic banks. No specific requirement exists in Japan and in the United States (7), where the granting of a licence is subject to the general criterion that the applicant must have sufficient financial strength to carry on banking business in a sound and efficient manner. Finally, in the United Kingdom, a branch of a foreign bank is not expected to maintain its own capital since it is regarded as an integral part of the total operation of the bank worldwide. However, the United Kingdom supervisory authorities will require confirmation from the supervisors of the home country of the parent bank that the capital adequacy of the bank is satisfactory.

No major complaints by banks have been reported as regards the fixing of minimum standards for branches' endowment capital. However, the use of the concept of branch capital, rather than the capital of the bank as a whole, in the calculation of gearing and other banking ratios for supervisory purposes is frequently perceived by the banking community as an important hindrance to the potential expansion of the branch's business.

Another potential source of discriminatory treatment arises from provisions on the nationality and competence of personnel. With regard to competence of managers and directors of foreign-owned banking institutions, they are generally subject to the same requirements applied to local banks. These provisions typically require that members of Boards of Directors and senior management are persons of integrity who have suitable experience in banking and the necessary professional qualifications. Although some of these requirements could be used to discriminate against foreign banks, as matters stand, it seems that their application aims basically at ensuring that management is carried out with the prudence and skill consistent with the maintenance of professional standards in the local market.

Non-residents controlling the operations of foreign-owned banking institutions are subject to the general provisions concerning foreigners working in the host country (eg. permanent address in the host country, working permits, etc.). However, a number of countries apply specific requirements as regards the nationality of directors or managers. Thus, Canada requires that one half of the Board of Directors of a foreign bank subsidiary must be Canadian citizens ordinarily resident in Canada. Three quarters of the Directors of any other bank must meet those criteria. In Finland, half of the members of the Board of Directors and of the Supervisory Board may be foreigners or Finnish citizens residing abroad. In principle, the management of a bank operating in France is confined to citizens of EEC states, but derogations are granted liberally by the Ministry of Finance. The majority of the members of the Board of Directors of any bank established in Greece must be of Greek nationality. In Ireland, a majority of the Board of Directors and of the local Supervisory Board may be required to be Irish or nationals of other EEC states, but in practice the Central Bank does not insist on strict compliance with nationality requirements. As for any company domiciled in Switzerland, the majority of the Board of Directors of a foreign bank must have Swiss nationality and residence. Finally, in the United States the International Banking Act permits up to one-half of the directors of a national bank to be foreign nationals. State laws may require that directors of state-licensed banks be United States citizens.

One important reason for applying specific requirements on the nationality of directors is to ensure that some members of senior management have adequate knowledge of local laws, regulations and market practices. It may also be noted that provisions for nationality apply generally to indigenous banks, too. By and large, the importance of this kind of restriction would appear to be minor, but in the case of a number of countries foreign banks complain about the difficulty of obtaining work permits for foreigners although they recognise that this is not a problem specific to the banking sector.

An area in which differential requirements apply to foreign-owned banks in a number of countries concerns the provisions of special guarantees and/or "letters of comfort" from the parent institution. In some cases (e.g. Canada, Finland, Ireland, the United Kingdom) the request for a letter of comfort has become an established practice as a means for obtaining a formal acknowledgment of the parent bank's moral commitment to support its foreign offshoot. In other countries, the possibility of requesting specific guarantees is left to the discretion of the licensing body (8). In view of the existing problems concerning the demarcation of responsibility in parent-affiliate relations, the request for formal guarantees from foreign parent institutions can hardly be seen as a discriminatory provision and indeed banks do not seem to regard such requests as impediments to entry in foreign markets.

The survey of regulatory requirements relating to the granting of banking licences to foreign organistions suggests that broadly speaking, where foreign bank entry is permitted, licensing procedures apply uniformly to all applicants. In practice, however, forms of discriminatory treatment may arise in countries where licensing authorities enjoy discretionary powers and/or the conditions for granting or refusing a licence are not embodied in specific statutory criteria. In these countries, lack of transparency may hinder foreign institutions and limit their capacity to gain access to the local market on the same footing as indigenous banks.

B. ACQUISITION BY FOREIGN BANKING ORGANISATIONS OF PARTICIPATIONS IN INDIGENOUS BANKS

The position of Member countries on foreign banks' access to the local market through the acquisition of participations in indigenous banks is set out in Table II and in Tables 2.1 and 2.2 of Annex II:

Table 2.1. Regulations restricting foreign acquisition of participations in indigenous banks

Table 2.2. Other provisions applying to foreign acquisition of indigenous banks.

Foreign access to the domestic banking system through equity participations in indigenous banks is subject to the general provisions applying to inward direct investment (9), or to sector-specific controls affecting the banking sector and a number of Member countries have lodged reservations for this purpose to the OECD Code of Liberalisation of Capital Movements. Thus, the acquisition of any participation is forbidden by law or not permitted under current policy in Australia (with the exception of minor participations of a portfolio investment nature) and Sweden and the establishment of subsidiaries through the acquisition of majority interests in an indigenous bank is not normally permitted in Finland, Greece, Norway, and Turkey. The reasons for forbidding or severely restricting non-resident acquisitions of majority holdings in indigenous banks are broadly the same as for limiting de-novo foreign entry. In Portugal, the acquisition of any participation was prohibited by law in 1977, but foreign participation was permitted in parabanking institutions (investment and leasing companies) and in regional development companies. The above-mentioned prohibition was removed by Decree Law No. 406 of 19 November 1983.

Even in countries where there is no specific provision prohibiting the transfer of control of indigenous banking concerns to non-residents, the scope for foreign access to the local banking sector may be limited by national anti-trust and merger legislation and/or by provisions requiring that significant changes in the ownership structure of locally-incorporated banks be authorised by a banking control body. The results of the survey suggest that such provisions apply, in principle, equally to both domestic and foreign banks. In practice, however, discriminatory treatment against foreign banks may arise in the actual application of such provisions, especially if there is lack of transparency in respect of the criteria used for assessing whether the transfer of control would endanger competition, lead to an undesirable development of the banking sector or be otherwise against the public interest.

C. OPERATIONS OF ESTABLISHED FOREIGN-OWNED BANKING ORGANISATIONS

The extent to which a foreign bank organisation authorised to operate in a national market can compete on an equal footing with domestic banks depends in the first instance on the non-discriminatory character of regulatory provisions applying to the conduct of banking business (10). The survey focused on possible discrimination against foreign-owned banks in three major areas covered in Tables 3.1 to 3.3 of Annex II:

Table 3.1.   Limitations on the expansion of foreign branch networks

Table 3.2.   Differential restrictions on the type of services that can be offered and on the range of activities in which foreign banks can engage

Table 3.3.   Other differential restrictions affecting foreign-owned banks.

Branching

With regard to possible limitations on the expansion of foreign banks' branch networks, the great majority of Member countries applies uniform treatment to domestic and foreign-owned banks. The only differences which emerged from the survey were the following:

In Australia, the authorities held by Banque Nationale de Paris and Bank of New Zealand Savings Bank are conditional in that they specify the points at which the respective banks may carry on banking business: the approval of the Treasurer (a Government Minister) is required for those banks to establish additional points of representation. The authority held by Bank of New Zealand is unconditional.

In Canada, subsidiaries of foreign banks are not permitted to open branches outside Canada. The main rationale for this prohibition is the authorities' desire that Canada should not be used as a pass-through for foreign banking operations. On the other hand, this provision limits the scope for foreign bank subsidiaries to attract foreign-currency funds by offering reserve-free bearer deposits via branches located abroad, although, as the Canadian authorities point out, foreign bank subsidiaries can receive reserve-free foreign currency deposits which their parent companies have raised abroad. It may also be noted that foreign bank subsidiaries, as any other Schedule B bank but unlike Canadian Schedule A banks, may open more than one branch in Canada only subject to authorisation from the Minister of Finance. In practice, however, the authorities encourage the opening of branches, especially if they may contribute to a better regional distribution of banking offices in Canada.

In Greece, authorisation is required for any expansion of branch networks by both domestic or foreign banks. These latter, however, are in practice allowed to operate branches only in the major towns.

Table II

ACQUISITION BY FOREIGN BANKING ORGANISATIONS
OF PARTICIPATIONS IN INDIGENOUS BANKS

AUSTRALIA	--	Forbidden under current policy
AUSTRIA	--	Licence required
BELGIUM	--	Mergers are subject to prior authorisation. The banking control authorities must be notified of any significant change in equity ownership
CANADA	--	For Schedule A banks, permitted up to 10 per cent of capital for each shareholder (maximum 25 per cent held by non-residents). Free for Schedule B banks
DEMARK	--	Permitted up to 30 per cent of share capital (but possibility of authorisation for higher percentages)
FINLAND	--	Non-resident ownership limited to 20 per cent of share capital (but possibility of authorisation for higher percentages)
FRANCE	--	Authorisation required by Conseil National du Crédit
GERMANY	--	Free, subject to Anti-trust law
GREECE	--	Permitted up to 40 per cent of share capital (but possibility of authorisation up to 51 per cent)
IRELAND	--	Subject to the same requirements as for establishment of foreign bank subsidiaries
ITALY	--	Free
JAPAN	--	Free up to 5 per cent of equity capital; authorisation by the Fair Trade Commission required for higher percentages
LUXEMBOURG	--	Free
NETHERLANDS	--	Free up to 5 per cent of voting shares; higher participations subject to a declaration of non-objection
NEW ZEALAND	--	Authorisation required for foreign acquisition of 25 per cent or more of equity of New Zealand incorporated banks
NORWAY	--	Free up to 10 per cent of share capital (but possibility of authorisation up to 25 per cent)
PORTUGAL	--	Forbidden by law in 1977, except participations in regional development companies and parabanking institutions. Prohibition eliminated by Decree Law No. 406 of 19 November 1983.
SPAIN	--	Subject to individual authorisation
SWEDEN	--	Forbidden
SWITZERLAND	--	Authorisation required for majority participations
TURKEY	--	Authorisation may be granted for participations between 10 and 49 per cent of share capital
UNITED KINGDOM	--	Free up to 15 per cent of share capital; higher participations are subject to supervisory approval by the Bank of England and controlling majority participations may be subject to investigation
UNITED STATES	--	Free up to 5 per cent of voting shares; for higher participations, Federal regulatory approval is required

In Spain, foreign bank subsidiaries are allowed to establish two branches in addition to the head office (this limitation does not apply to local distressed banks taken over by foreign interests). Since foreign banks were allowed to re-enter the Spanish market only in 1978 after a 40-year ban, a limitation on branching authority was felt desirable to limit the risk of excessive competition by new restraints in a market which was regarded as already overbanked in some respect. The existing constraints on branching has limited the scope for foreign banks' inroads into the retail deposit market and has resulted in strong concentration of foreign banks' activities in the wholesale market.

In Turkey, foreign-owned banks can operate a maximum of five branches with only one branch permitted in each town; however, two branches may be opened in Istanbul, the one on the Anatolian side the other one on the European side.

Types of Services and Range of Activities

The results of the survey indicate that in Member countries there exist only a few regulatory provisions concerning the scope of banking authority which intentionally discriminate against foreign banks (see Table III).

Spain is the only Member country applying important discriminatory provisions on foreign banks' deposit-taking business (11). Thus, funds raised on the domestic market by a foreign bank licensed to operate in Spain under the Decree of 1978 may not exceed 40 per cent of the bank's total assets, unless a special authorisation is granted by the Central bank. The ceiling does not include funds raised on the Spanish inter-bank market. This limitation was introduced at the time of reopening the Spanish banking sector to foreign banks in order to moderate the impact of foreign bank entry on competition for domestic deposits. Although the effect of this requirement is mitigated by a favourable treatment for foreign banks with regard to the possibility of extending avals and guarantees, it represents an effective limitation to their competitiveness.

Discriminatory restraints exist in the field of security business in a number of countries. In principle, the security portfolio of foreign banks operating in Spain may consist only of government securities and private bonds, though authorisation may be granted for the holding of equity participations in companies operating in certain areas of the financial services industry. In Austria, foreign banks are normally not permitted to issue bonds and manage, or participate in, security issues. In a number of other countries (e.g. France, Germany, Netherlands, Switzerland), the lead management of domestic currency issues is confined to domestic banks by administrative practice; in the United Kingdom, foreign banks are eligible to participate in leading sterling issues if they have the appropriate issuing house capacity in London and reciprocal opportunities for United Kingdom banks exist in their domestic markets.

Other Differential Operating Provisions

The survey covered a wide range of areas where differential treatment between domestic and foreign-owned banks could arise from regulatory provisions or administrative practices (see items 3.3 to 3.9 of Annex I). In examining the extent to which National Treatment is applied in these areas, only a very few instances of potential discrimination against foreign banks. This is presently the case for Finland with regard to recently-established banks' access to some Central Bank facilities; Austria in respect of government insurance for export financing (12); and Greece as far as the repatriation of profits is concerned.

Another special issue arises in the case of Canada. The Canadian Bank Act distinguishes between two types of banks: widely-held banks (Schedule A) and closely-held banks (Schedule B). Since they are closely held, foreign bank subsidiaries can only belong to the latter class of banks. In principle, regulatory provisions apply equally to all Schedule B banks, whether domestic or foreign-owned, but they may differ between Schedule A and Schedule B banks. As a result, foreign banks operating in Canada have argued that, although they are put on the same footing as Canadian Schedule B banks, there is a lack of National Treatment insofar as they are put at a disadvantage vis-à-vis Schedule A banks. In particular, they have expressed concern about administrative guidance related to funding offshore of Canadian dollar assets, the sale of assets by foreign bank subsidiaries to their parent institution, and assets to capital ratios. Foreign bank subsidiaries have been requested not to fund more than 50 per cent of their Canadian dollar assets offshore (Schedule A banks, on the other hand, fund less than 3 per cent of their domestic assets with offshore funds). In the view of the Canadian authorities, the lack of National Treatment constitutes more favourable treatment accorded foreign banks' subsidiaries, for the following reasons:

a) With respect to assets to capital rations, limitations relate directly to prudential considerations;

b) Smaller banks, both domestic and foreign-owned, are permitted lower assets to capital ratios than larger banks;

c) There is no National Treatment issue with respect to the sale of assets to parent institutions since the circumstance does not arise in the case of Schedule A banks.

The material provided by the BIAC Committee on Capital Movements and Capital Markets suggests that the most important group of obstacles does not concern provisions and requirements that intentionally discriminate against foreign banks but, rather, a set of regulatory provisions that apply uniformly across-the-board but bear more heavily on foreign institutions because of differences in balance-sheet structures. Although such impediments do not constitute a breach of National Treatment, they may influence the competitive balance as between foreign and domestic banks. This is also an area where foreign bankers are quick to detect unequal treatment without giving sufficient weight to such balance-sheet differences. The Committee envisages to undertake further work in this area in the next stage of the exercise.

Table III

RESTRICTIONS ON THE TYPE OF SERVICES THAT CAN BE OFFERED AND ON THE RANGE OF ACTIVITIES IN WHICH FOREIGN BANKS CAN ENGAGE

	Solicitations of deposits from the public	Access to public authorities' deposits	Lending to residents	Investment in securities	Access to local money markets	Management of and participation in security issues	Foreign exchange transactions	Issuance of bonds by banks	Acquisition of equity participations in domestic enterprises
AUSTRALIA									
AUSTRIA									
BELGIUM									
CANADA									
DENMARK									
FINLAND									
FRANCE						r			
GERMANY						r			a
GREECE									
IRELAND									
ITALY									
JAPAN									
LUXEMBOURG									
NETHERLANDS									
NEW ZEALAND									
NORWAY						r			
PORTUGAL									
SPAIN									
SWEDEN	X			X		X		X	X
SWITZERLAND	NA	NA	NA		NA		NA		
TURKEY									
UNITED KINGDOM		a							
UNITED STATES		(x)							

NA: not applicable because foreign bank presence is prohibited
X: regulatory provisions of a discriminatory nature
r: restraints arising from administrative practices
a: activity requiring special authorisation
(x): access to state deposits
(%): subject to overall ceiling

D. CROSS-BORDER INTERNATIONAL BANKING OPERATIONS

Part III of Annex II presents a survey of limitations on market access by banks operating from outside the country (13). The survey focused on three categories of international capital transactions involving foreign-based banks, namely:

    i) Holding of deposits by residents at foreign-based banks;

    ii) Borrowing by residents from foreign-based banks;

    iii) Holding of deposits by non-resident banks with resident banks.

Only seven Member countries (Belgium, Canada, Germany, Luxembourg, Switzerland, United Kingdom and the United States) apply no restriction or authorisation requirement to these categories of international operations. In all other countries there are impediments of varying importance and coverage resulting from exchange control provisions. It is to be noted, however, that such restraints are not primarily motivated by the intention to discriminate against the activities of foreign-based banks. Generally, they are introduced and maintained for balance-of-payments reasons, to ensure a certain degree of monetary autonomy and to achieve other general macro-economic policy goals. This being said, the importance of such obstacles to international banking activity is evident.

In Switzerland, and perhaps in other countries, banks that are not domiciled in the country are not allowed to participate in syndicates for the issue on the domestic market of securities denominated in the national currency. The main motivation behind such a requirement is to be found in the authorities' desire to keep control over the international use of the national currency. Although this provision may be viewed as discriminatory, a justification for their application exists insofar as the country concerned allows foreign banks to have a physical presence in the domestic banking system, thereby enabling them to participate in the issuing syndicate.

The Committee's Expert Group on Banking held a preliminary and limited exchange of views on possible obstacles to the provision to residents by banks located abroad of other banking services such as credit cards, portfolio management and so on. To the extent that such operations do not imply a transfer of funds, they do not fall within the scope of exchange control provisions. Therefore, restraints in their regard must be motivated by other factors, possibly including discriminatory considerations. The Committee considers that this area would deserve to be explored further in view of the potential importance of restrictions on the provision of international financial services.

E. CONCLUSIONS REGARDING THE ANALYSIS AND ASSESSMENT OF OBSTACLES

Any classification of identified obstacles by order of importance has its limitations. It would, nevertheless, appear from the above review of obstacles that, as far as Member countries are concerned, the most serious impediments relate to limitations to the granting of right of establishment to foreign-owned banks. Current regulations and policies provide scope for some foreign banking presence in all Member countries; but in a number of instances, the right of establishment of "operative" bank offshoots (agencies, branches, subsidiaries) is either not granted or is severely limited.

The importance of limitations to right of establishment in the banking sector may be somewhat attenuated if possibilities exist for foreign banks to provide financial services to residents of a given country either through offshore operations or by operating in the domestic market through local establishments that are not considered to be "banks" according to national legislation. It remains true, however, that access to the local market through authorisation to have a physical, operative presence is a prerequisite to the pursuit of banking business proper.

Restrictions on aspects of establishment other than licensing per se (e.g. reciprocity considerations, special authorisation modalities, differential licensing requirements) may severely affect foreign banks' ability to compete on equal footing with domestic institutions. Although the number of discriminatory provisions in this area would appear to be fairly limited, hindrances to the establishment of foreign banks often arise from administrative practices, the importance of which may be compounded by lack of transparency.

It is difficult to form an opinion of the extent to which existing restraints on the acquisition of participations in indigenous banks effectively limit the scope for international trade in banking services. No doubt, the severest impact of such restraints is felt in those countries which concurrently prohibit or severely restrict de-novo entry. On the other hand, countries applying a liberal policy with regard to de-novo entry offer foreign banks a viable alternative to the establishment in the local market via the acquisition of indigenous banks. Finally, a large number of Member countries allow foreign banks to take minority participations in local institutions. This may provide foreign banks with an opportunity for complementing and strengthening their correspondent network and for the provision of services to customers in countries where a full-scale presence would not necessarily be warranted.

The results of the survey suggest that when foreign institutions are admitted as fully-fledged banks, Member countries generally apply National Treatment to them and only a few instances are noted in this survey where such is not the case. Of significantly greater importance for the competitive position of foreign banks may be the effect of a number of regulatory provisions which, although formally applied in a uniform manner to all financial institutions operating in a country, in practice bear more heavily on foreign banks than on their local competitors.

In the field of cross-border transactions, the numerous impediments that exist in a number of countries are not generally intended to discriminate against non-resident banks and usually result from measures governments have taken in pursuit of other policy objectives. It remains, however, that they may run contrary to the principle of liberalisation of capital movements and, in practical terms, may limit severely market access by foreign banking institutions. Moreover, there are obstacles to the provision of certain financial services outside traditional international capital transactions (e.g. credit cards, portfolio management) which are likely to be protectionist in intent, at least to a certain degree.

Section II

OECD INVESTMENT INSTRUMENTS AND OBSTACLES TO
INTERNATIONAL BANKING OPERATIONS

Existing OECD investment instruments cover, in varying degrees, all the four areas in which restraints on international banking operations may arise as a result of either legal restrictions or discriminatory administrative practices. The following paragraphs are designed to provide a review of the coverage of the existing instruments and to indicate briefly in which direction work in the relevant OECD Committees is currently evolving.

A. DE-NOVO ENTRY AND ESTABLISHMENT OF FOREIGN BANKING ORGANISATIONS

There are two major issues relating to the de-novo entry and establishment of foreign banking institutions, namely the application of the concept of right of establishment, and the implications of the principle of reciprocity as applied by a number of Member countries.

Direct investment in banking is liberalised under the Code of Liberalisation of Capital Movements (item I/A of Annex A) and Member countries have an obligation to grant any authorisation required for the conclusion of execution of transactions and for transfers unless a Member has a specific dispensation in the form of a reservation or a temporary derogation.

With regard to the issue of right of establishment, it should be noted that establishment conditions are explicitly excluded from the scope of the National Treatment instrument. Thus, the Declaration on International Investment and Multinational Enterprises adopted by the governments of OECD Member countries on 21st June 1976, states that "this Declaration does not deal with the right of Member countries to regulate the entry of foreign investment or the conditions of establishment of foreign enterprises" (art. II, 4).

The Code of Liberalisation of Capital Movements and the Code of Liberalisation of Current Invisible Operations deal with banking operations in a particular manner. A number of medium-term international banking operations are liberalised under the Capital Movements Code, but the Current Invisibles Code does not include a specific section on banking as it does for other services sectors such as insurance, maritime transports, etc. Most of right-of-establishment issues are currently excluded from the coverage of the OECD liberalisation codes. The entry in the Council Minutes relating to their adoption notes that "the Code of Liberalisation of Current Invisible Operations and the Code of Liberalisation of Capital Movements did not confer the right of establishment unless an item in their annexes expressly provides for that right" (14). In fact, the Code of Liberalisation of Current Invisible Operations does not generally cover the right of establishment except for some items such as the establishment of insurance branches or agencies.

Concerning the Capital Movements Code, the Committee on Capital Movements and Invisible Transactions (CMIT) has submitted a report to the Council on the application of that code to inward direct investment dealing with certain aspects of the right of establishment. The CMIT is presently considering whether those aspects of the right of establishment most directly connected with direct investment should be covered in the Capital Movements Code in order to reach a standardised treatment of Member countries' positions under that code.

The issue of reciprocity is now being addressed explicitly by the CMIT in its current review of the application of the Code of Liberalisation of Current Invisible Transactions and an inquiry has been completed as regards the insurance sector where similar provisions exist. The CMIT is aware of the divergence between such provisions and the principle of non-discrimination enshrined in both Codes of Liberalisation and is aware also of the fact that the reciprocity principle also exists in the banking sector. The CMIT is expecting progress of the work in this sector to see how the issues raised by that divergence could be settled in the event of an extension of the coverage of the Codes to a number of establishment issues.

B. ACQUISITION BY FOREIGN BANKING ORGANISATIONS OF PARTICIPATIONS IN INDIGENOUS BANKS

The acquisition of participations by non-residents in locally-charted banks is liberalised under the Code of Liberalisation of Capital Movements (15), as are all direct investment operations, and Member countries have an obligation to grant any authorisation required for the conclusion of execution of transactions and for transfers, unless a Member has a specific dispensation in the form of a reservation or a temporary derogation. As noted previously, however, purely administrative conditions placed on the establishment of banks are currently not covered by the provisions of the Capital Movements Code (16). The on-going CMIT exercise on the application of the Code to inward direct investment -- which relates, inter alia, to the issue of establishment conditions -- should help by getting certain licensing and regulatory measures reported and covered by reservations where they bear more heavily on foreign financial institutions.

C. OPERATIONS OF ESTABLISHED FOREIGN-OWNED BANKING ORGANISATIONS

The OECD Declaration on International Investment and Multinational Enterprises of 1976 includes a National Treatment instrument providing that "Member countries should ... accord to enterprises operating in their territories and owned or controlled directly or indirectly by nationals of another Member country treatment under their laws, regulations and administrative practices, consistent with international law and no less favourable than that accorded in like situations to domestic enterprises". Measures constituting exceptions to National Treatment must be notified to the Organisation. The Committee on International Investment and Multinational Enterprises (CIME) has been entrusted with a review of the application of National Treatment and the examination of national exceptions to it. A first survey of exceptions has been published in 1978 (17). The scope and extent of application of the instrument has been progressively clarified in recent years (17). On this basis and with a view to increasing the transparency of government policies as applied to foreign-controlled enterprises, work is underway in the CIME aiming at updating the 1978 survey and at extending it to measures related to national treatment that do not constitute exceptions to National Treatment. Work is also underway concerning the motivations for those measures and the relative importance of their effects.

With regard to banking, a first study concerning, inter alia, some issues relating to branching and to regulatory provisions concerning the activities of financial institutions is nearing completion. It is expected that some of these issues may require further consideration in the light of information to be provided by Member countries in the context of the updating of exceptions to National Treatment and of information made available through the present CMF exercise.

D. CROSS-BORDER INTERNATIONAL BANKING OPERATIONS

Cross-border transactions by banks and other financial institutions are subject to the liberalisation provisions set out in the Current Invisibles Code and the Capital Movements Code. The latter is particularly relevant for a number of operations, usually involving the activities of the banking sector, such as commercial and financial credit, portfolio operations, etc. It is worth noting, however, that the coverage of the Capital Movements Code does not extend to a number of operations of particular importance for banks, such as buying and selling of short-term securities normally dealt in on the money market (item VII of the General List of International Capital Movements); most short-term (less than one year) and certain medium- and long-term financial credits and loans (item IX); and all operations of accounts with credit institutions (item X), including, in particular, deposit operations. The logic behind this exclusion in the Code was, at the time of its adoption, that the movement of short-term funds belonged to the domain of domestic monetary policy. This approach may have lost some of its justification today and require re-examination. Since 1978, the Committee on Financial Markets has undertaken to gather information on country regulations pertaining to international capital transactions. Such information, covering both exchange control measures and other relevant regulatory provisions, has been published in the series "Regulations Affecting International Banking Operations".

NOTES AND REFERENCES

1. The two OECD Codes of Liberalisation of Current Invisible Transactions and Capital Movements and the instrument on National Treatment.

2. The reader is referred to the monograph The Internationalisation of Banking, OECD, Paris 1984, Chapter III, Section B.

3. Representative offices are extensions of the parent bank with no separate legal status which are usually not considered as "banking entities" under the host country's banking legislation. Agencies and branches have also no separate legal status. They are simply extensions of the parent bank whose name they bear, with authority to carry on banking business. By contrast, subsidiaries are banking off-shoots incorporated under local law, with the nationality of the host country, which are controlled by a foreign bank according to the host country's definitions.

4. In some instances, state laws do not expressly permit the establishment of such offices. In this case, the Comptroller of the Currency may licence a federal agency or branch in that state, provided that the state is the foreign bank's "home state" under the rules of the International Banking Act.

5. The licence of foreign bank subsidiary in Canada must be renewed annually for the first five years and every three years thereafter. This procedure is motivated by the authorities' desire to check the foreign bank's compliance with Canadian bank regulations and the maintenance of reciprocal treatment in the parent bank's home country.

6. Thus, entry of foreign subsidiaries must be authorised by the Council of Ministers in Finland, Spain and Turkey.

7. However, federally-licensed branches of foreign banks are subject to a statutory requirement for a 5 per cent asset pledge.

8. It is noteworthy that in Italy the provision of a letter of comfort is not compulsory for branches of EEC banks but the lack of such a guarantee entails a limitation in the foreign branch's operational powers.

9. For details, see Controls and Impediments Affecting Inward Direct Investment in OECD Member countries, OECD, 1982.

10. Information is available in National Treatment of Foreign-controlled Enterprises Established in OECD Countries, OECD, 1978. This information is in the process of being up-dated.

11. In the United States access to state government and other state public authorities' deposits by foreign banks is determined by individual state authorities. In the United Kingdom, foreign banks may have access to government deposits upon request. Finally, in Germany branches of foreign banks may not act for prudential reasons as banks of deposit for mutual funds of German investment companies. Such a restriction does not apply to foreign bank subsidiaries.

12. Foreign banks may participate in export financing upon request.

13. Additional information can be found in Regulations Affecting International Banking Operations, OECD, 1981, Volumes I and II. See also Code of Liberalisation of Capital Movements, OECD, 1982.

14. OECD, Acts of the Organisation, Volume I, p. 477.

15. Under item 1/A (Direct Investment) of Annex A (Liberalisation Lists of Capital Movements) of the Capital Movements Code, Member countries undertake to liberalise "investment for the purpose of establishing lasting economic relations with an undertaking such as, in particular, investments which give the possibility of exercising an effective influence on the management thereof, in the country concerned by non-residents by means of:

    1. .... acquisition of full ownership of an existing enterprise;

    2. participation in a new or existing enterprise."

    If the acquisition of participation is of a "portfolio capital" nature, it is subject to the liberalisation requirements set out under item IV/A1 in List A and IV/A3 in List B (Buying and Selling of Securities) of Annex A.

16. The Capital Movements Code provides, however, that "if a Member considers that the measures of liberalisation ... are frustrated by internal arrangements likely to restrict the possibility of effecting transactions or transfers ... it may refer to the Organisation" which "... may make suitable suggestions with regard to the removal or modifications of such arrangements" (art. 16). To date, no use has been made of such procedure.

17. For a recent review of the work by the CIME with regard to the National Treatment instrument, see International Investment and Multinational Enterprises: Mid-term Report on the 1976 Declaration and Decisions, OECD, 1982, Chapter II.

A N N E X E S

Annex I

QUESTIONNAIRE ON POSSIBLE OBSTACLES TO INTERNATIONAL BANKING OPERATIONS

I. ENTRY, ESTABLISHMENT AND MARKET ACCESS

1. Entry and establishment of foreign banking organisations

    1.1. Regulatory provisions governing the entry and establishment by foreign banks of:

    -- representative offices

    -- branches

    -- wholly-owned subsidiaries

    -- majority-owned subsidiaries

    N.B. In detailing the provisions applicable to foreign institutions, please indicate the extent to which they differ from provisions applied to domestic banks.

    1.2. Reciprocity provisions that apply against foreign states and regions

    1.3. Impediments deriving from policy or administrative practices (including special licensing procedures)

    1.4. Requirements for earmarked capital applying to branches of foreign banks

    1.5. Restrictions on who can own a bank

    1.6. Regulatory and administrative provisions on nationality, language requirements, and competence of personnel and management

    1.7. Requirement of guarantees and "letters of comfort" from parent institutions

    1.8. Restrictions on foreign bank entry by sub-national political units (e.g. states, regions, etc.).

2. Acquisitions of participations in indigenous banks

    2.1. Regulations restricting foreign acquisition of participations in indigenous banks

    2.2. Reciprocity provisions that apply against foreign states and regions

    2.3. Impediments deriving from policy and administrative practices

    N.B. Please indicate maximum foreign participation allowed in practice.

    2.4. Restraints deriving from regulations concerning mergers in the banking sector

    2.5. Restrictions on who can own a bank

    2.6. Provision on nationality of directors

    2.7. Requirements of guarantees from investing institutions

    2.8. Restrictions on the foreign acquisition of participations in indigenous banks by sub-national political units (e.g. states, regions, etc.).

II. DOMESTIC OPERATIONS OF ESTABLISHED FOREIGN-OWNED BANKING ORGANISATIONS

    3.1. Limitations on the expansion of foreign branch networks, including administrative practices that bear more heavily upon foreign branches

    3.2. Restrictions on the type of services that can be offered and on the range of activities in which foreign banks can engage as compared with domestic banks. In particular, please provide details of restrictions (either from regulations or administrative practices) on:

        a)   Solicitation of deposits from the public;

        b)   access to government and other public authorities' deposits;

        c)   lending to domestic residents;

        d)   investment in securities;

        e)   access to local money markets;

        f)   management of and participation in security issues;

        g)   foreign exchange transactions;

        h)   issuance of bonds by banks;

i)   acquisition of equity participation in domestic financial and non-financial enterprises.

3.3. Restrictions on advertising and soliciting of customers

3.4. Governmental or administrative prudential controls applied to foreign-owned banks where different from those applied to domestic-owned banks

Please provide details on the extent to which prudential supervision is applied in a differential manner to foreign-owned banks (including branches of foreign banks)

3.5. Non-prudential regulations (e.g. consumer protection; regulations on data transmission) applied to foreign-owned banks where different

3.6. Special tax measures and regimes applied to foreign-owned banks

3.7. Limitations on access by foreign-owned banks to government aids or measures

In particular:

-- access to subsidised funds for export financing

-- availability of government deposit insurance

-- access to government insurance for export financing

3.8. Monetary policy requirements applying to foreign-owned banks where different from domestic banks

In particular:

-- access to the discount window

-- discriminatory reserve requirements

-- discriminatory credit ceilings

3.9. Other types of restrictions on foreign-owned banks

In particular:

-- government procurement

-- limitations on repatriation of profits or funds

-- obstacles to trade in goods necessary to banking services (e.g. computers)

-- obstacles in gaining access to courts or regulatory bodies, or biased procedures once access has been obtained

-- private restrictive practices

-- obstacles in gaining access to deposit insurance systems run by
   domestic banking organisations.

III. INTERNATIONAL BANKING OPERATIONS (CROSS-REFERENCE MAY BE MADE TO RELEVANT PARTS OF THE 1981 REPORT REGULATIONS AFFECTING INTERNATIONAL BANKING OPERATIONS, VOLS. I AND II)

4.   Capital and foreign exchange controls which impede non-resident banks
     from conducting business with residents.

5.   Other limitations on market access by banks operating from outside of
     the country.

Annex II

DESCRIPTION OF IMPEDIMENTS

Part I

ENTRY, ESTABLISHMENT AND MARKET ACCESS

Table 1.1

REGULATORY PROVISIONS GOVERNING THE ENTRY
AND ESTABLISHMENT OF FOREIGN BANKS (*)

AUSTRALIA -- It has been longstanding Australian Government policy not to grant to foreign interests authority to carry on the general business of banking in Australia (1).

-- Generally, the Australian Government has not refused requests by foreign banks to establish representative offices in Australia for business liaison purposes. A foreign bank is required to provide an undertaking that it will not use its representative office to engage in any form of banking business or any financial transaction other than whatever might be necessary for, and incidental to, the maintenance of its office.

-- Under current government foreign investment policy, proposals by foreign banks to establish a new non-bank financial intermediary are closely examined by the Foreign Investment Review Board which makes recommendations to the Treasurer. Current policy provides that such proposals must show substantial net economic benefits to Australia or, where the economic benefits are small, must involve an effective partnership between Australian interests and the foreign investor in the ownership and control of the company concerned.

---

* This Table summarises answers to item 1.1 of the questionnaire.

-- In January 1983 the then Government announced that it had decided, in principle, to allow for the initial entry of around 10 banks with foreign shareholdings into the Australian banking system. However, on 5th March a general election resulted in a change of government. The new Government announced on 29th May that it had commissioned a small group (the Martin Group) to prepare a report on the structure of the financial system, including the question of foreign bank entry. The Group's terms of reference stated that the report should have regard to the recommendations of the earlier Committee of Inquiry into the Australian financial system, and take into account the Government's economic and social objectives as well as the need to improve the efficiency of the financial system. The report was completed towards the end of 1983, and its recommendations are currently subject to the Government's consideration.

AUSTRIA
-- No licence is required for the establishment of a representative office of a foreign bank.

-- Branches of foreign banks are considered as legally independent banking organisations and as such a licence is required for their establishment. If a foreign bank maintains several branches in Austria they are treated as one bank. A licence is denied in those cases where the legal provisions in the home country of the foreign bank do not warrant the observance of the Austrian Banking Law.

-- The opening of foreign-owned subsidiaries is subject to the same provisions applied to Austrian banks.

BELGIUM
-- The opening of representative offices is subject to the authorisation by the Banking Commission which is usually granted, provided the office is not used for carrying on banking business or for soliciting business to be channelled through offices outside Belgium.

-- Regulatory provisions governing the entry and establishment of branches and subsidiaries apply equally to both Belgian and foreign banks.

-- In the case of establishment of branches by a foreign bank, the conditions applicable to banks incorporated in Belgium apply equally to the parent institutions:

a) The parent institution must carry on banking business (as defined in the Decree No. 185 of 1935);

b) The parent institution must be a "société commerciale" (a commercial company) with legal personality.

CANADA
-- Foreign banks are permitted to have representative offices in Canada, provided such offices are registered and operated in the manner prescribed by Regulation. There are annual fees and reporting requirements pertaining to such offices.

-- Foreign banks are not permitted to have branches in Canada.

-- The Bank Act provides for the establishment of two classes of banks. Schedule A banks are those that were chartered when the Act came into force together with new banks which are established later and whose shares are widely held. For new Schedule A banks, no one shareholder or group of associated shareholders will, after a possible transitional period, be permitted to own more than 10 per cent of the bank's voting shares. By contrast, Schedule B banks are permitted to be closely-held upon incorporation and include subsidiaries of foreign banks. Under the provisions of the British North America Act, the Federal Parliament has exclusive power to regulate banking in Canada. As a result, all chartered banks are established and regulated under the Bank Act which provides for the powers, restrictions and obligations applicable to such chartered banks. Though there are a range of institutions undertaking various types of lending and borrowing in Canada, including the acceptance of deposits transferable by order, generally only those institutions cited in Schedules A or B to the Bank Act are "banks" and are allowed to describe their business that of "banking".

-- The size of the domestic operations of the foreign bank sector is restricted to 8 per cent of total domestic assets of all banks in Canada as shown in Schedule Q of the Bank Act. Domestic assets of a foreign bank subsidiary may not exceed twenty times its deemed authorised capital.

DENMARK   -- There are no provisions concerning the establishment of representative offices.

-- The entry and establishment of foreign banking organisations is, in principle, subject to the same provisions applied to Danish banks. Banks from the other Member States of the European Communities are granted a right of entry and establishment as a consequence of Danish membership. Applications from banks from other countries are judged on a case by case basis and one of the fundamental considerations is whether reciprocity exists as regards Danish banks' establishment in the country concerned.

-- Banks from the other Member countries of the EEC must obtain permission from the Government Supervisor of Commercial Banks and Savings Banks to establish a branch in Denmark, whereas the establishment of branches of banks from other countries requires the permission of the Minister for Industry. The latter grants the permission for the investment, including the amount, according to the general rules on direct investment in Denmark (Executive Order No. 148 of 18th March 1981).

-- The establishment of wholly-owned or majority-owned subsidiaries of foreign banks is subject to the same rules as for Danish banks. Establishment always requires permission from the Government Supervisor and the investment of the capital from abroad requires permission from the Minister for Industry.

FINLAND — Foreign banks and other credit institutions are allowed to establish representative offices, wholly-owned banking subsidiaries, and majority-owned subsidiaries in Finland (Act. No. 684/78 in force as from 1st January 1979). Foreign banks are not allowed to establish branches.

— A permit from the Ministry of Finance is required for the establishment of a representative office.

— The Ministry of Finance may authorise a foreigner or a foreign bank or another credit institution to establish a banking joint venture.

— The Council of State (the Government) may for particular reasons grant a foreign bank or other foreign credit institution licence to establish a wholly-owned banking subsidiary or a majority-owned subsidiary where ownership exceeds 20 per cent of the share capital. A foreign bank can be a commercial bank, mortgage bank or a credit company, which are legally joint-stock companies. Therefore the provisions of the Finnish banking legislation and the new company law are applicable to the foreign-owned banks. Thus the legal position of a foreign-owned bank and a domestic bank is the same.

FRANCE — Any institution, either French or foreign, carrying on the general business of banking must obtain a licence from the Conseil National du Crédit. As in the case of domestic banks, the granting of a licence to foreign-owned establishments is subject to specific requirements concerning the legal form of the institution (banks are not allowed to operate as partnerships with limited liability -- sociétés à responsabilité limité -- or as "sociétés à capital variable"); minimum capitalisation; general economic needs; and the reputability of the managers. In addition, the establishment of foreign banks is subject to the general exchange control provisions applying to foreign direct investment.

— The opening of representative offices of foreign banks does not require prior authorisation.

GERMANY — The entry and establishment of business entities in the Federal Republic of Germany by foreign banks is generally governed by the same regulatory provisions as apply to domestic banks.

— Representative offices of foreign banks do not need a licence; their establishment, relocation and closing must, however, be reported to the Federal Banking Supervisory Office and the Deutsche Bundesbank.

— Branches of foreign banks are deemed to be banks (if a foreign bank maintains several branches in the Federal Republic of Germany they are treated as one bank). They are subject to the same licensing requirements as German banks, with two exceptions in the case of non-EEC banks:

     i) A separate licence is required for each branch of the foreign bank;

    ii) The licence may be refused if its granting is not justified in the light of general economic needs. So far, however, no licence has ever been denied to a branch of a foreign bank on these grounds.

-- Wholly-owned subsidiaries and majority-owned subsidiaries are regarded in law as German banks. There are no entry barriers. As in the case of German-owned banks, a licence may be refused to them only:

    -- If the resources necessary for conducting business -- in particular adequate liable capital -- are not available;

    -- If facts are known which indicate that an applicant or one of the managers is not trustworthy;

    -- If facts are known which indicate that the proprietor of a partnership or one of the managers does not have the professional qualifications necessary for managing the bank;

    -- If the bank does not have at least two managers who work for it in more than an honorary capacity.

GREECE   -- Prior specific approval by the monetary authorities is required for the establishment of a representative office or a new branch.

    -- The establishment of foreign-owned subsidiaries is subject to the same procedures applying to the establishment of any new bank in Greece, i.e. monetary authorities' approval, legal form of Société Anonyme with minimum, fully paid-up, capital of Dr 1 billion.

IRELAND   -- The establishment of foreign banks' branches or subsidiaries is subject to the Central Bank's licensing requirements. Such requirements (including minimum capital, ownership structure, composition of board and management, net national benefits likely to arise from the proposed establishment) apply uniformly to all applicants.

    -- An applicant for a bank licence from within the EEC must be an authorised credit institution (within the meaning of the EEC Banking Directive of 1977) having separate own funds or a company constituted under the laws of a Member State of the EEC and having a legal form acceptable to the Central Bank.

    -- An applicant for a licence from outside the EEC may be required to incorporate locally in a legal form acceptable to the Central Bank and what is deemed by the Central Bank to be an appreciable part of the share capital may be required to be in beneficial Irish ownership. However, banking corporations of standing may be permitted to establish on a branch or wholly-owned subsidiary basis. In practice, the decision to establish a branch or subsidiary in the case of such corporations is largely left to the corporation itself.

-- The establishment of representative offices of foreign banks requires prior approval by the Central Bank.

ITALY
-- No authorisation is required for the opening of a foreign bank's representative office.

-- The opening of branches of both Italian and foreign banks is subject to prior authorisation. In the case of non-EEC banks, authorisation is granted in accordance with Royal Decree No. 1620 of 1919. A decree is issued by the Treasury Minister, in agreement with the Minister of Foreign Affairs, after consulting the International Committee for Credit and Saving. The authorisation is subject to the proviso that the principle of reciprocity is respected. As for EEC banks, under the terms of a resolution of the Interministerial Committee for Credit and Saving, the Banca d'Italia grants the necessary authorisation in accordance with Article 28 of the Banking Law. The principle applied is that of "non-discrimination".

-- As regards the establishment of subsidiaries, there is a directive of a general nature (issued by the Interministerial Committee for Credit and Saving on 23rd June 1966) that suspended the establishment of new commercial banks. Derogations to this directive have been granted exceptionally in the case of banks being set up with mixed (Italian and foreign) capital.

JAPAN
-- The establishment of a representative office requires prior notification to the Minister of Finance which, if it is deemed necessary, may require that the parent bank submit reports or material concerning the activities to be conducted by the representative office.

-- A foreign bank wishing to engage in banking in Japan through a branch or an agency must designate a representative and obtain a banking licence from the Minister of Finance. The granting of the licence is subject to the same provisions (adequacy of resources; competence of personnel; general economic needs) applying to Japanese banks. However, reciprocity considerations may also apply.

-- The setting up of a wholly-owned or majority-owned subsidiary requires a licence from the Ministry of Finance which is granted on the same basis as for domestic banks though reciprocity considerations may also apply.

LUXEMBOURG
-- The entry and establishment of foreign banking organisations are subject to the same provisions as for domestic banks.

NETHERLANDS -- No regulatory provisions apply to the entry and establishment by foreign banks of representative offices.

-- As an enterprise or institution is only permitted to engage in the business of a credit institution after it has received a licence to do so from De Nederlandsche Bank, branches, wholly-owned subsidiaries and majority-owned subsidiaries established by foreign banks have to apply to the Bank to grant them a licence. A licence will be granted to credit institutions which meet three specific requirements (minimum amount of "own resources"; requirements for the person in charge of day-to-day management; and certification of the annual accounts) which apply equally to both foreign and domestic institutions.

-- A credit institution which has obtained a licence shall be entered in the register. Additionally, to complement the licensing system, unregistered institutions are prohibited from approaching the public for the purpose of soliciting deposits below Gld 100 000; and no one is allowed to act as an intermediary in the obtainment of such deposits by unregistered institutions. After consultation with the Bank, the Minister of Finance may grant exemption from the above prohibitions attaching certain conditions if necessary.

-- Under the Act the use of the word "bank" is reserved for a limited group of institutions: the institutions registered according to the Act on the Supervision of the Credit System. After consultation with the Bank, the Minister may grant exemption from the prohibition. The prohibition does not apply to the institutions from other EEC Member States which operate in the Netherlands and are entitled to use the word "bank" in their home country. The Bank may require an explanatory addition in respect of their legal status and the nature of their activity and financial position to the name used in this country. Exemption from the prohibition is given to representative offices of foreign banks if the parent bank is permitted to use the word "bank" and to engage in the business of a credit institution in its own country.

NEW ZEALAND -- Representative offices of foreign banks are permitted, with no effective restrictions except those defining the nature of a representative office.

-- At present, new foreign bank entry in the form of branches or subsidiaries of commercial banks would require both Overseas Investment Commission approval and special legislation.

-- The entry of foreign merchant banks is subject to the approval of the Overseas Investment Commission. Although the criteria used by the Commission are not hard and fast, factors considered include:

a) Whether a prospective entrant can offer services or expertise which are judged to be required in New Zealand;

42

b) The operating record of the prospective entrant, in terms of capital structure, expertise demonstrated, prudential aspects, etc.;

c) The extent of domestic equity participation in the proposed venture (generally restricted to a minimum of 50 per cent, although it can be less if other considerations warrant);

d) The usefulness to New Zealand of any network of overseas connections brought in by a new entrant.

NORWAY
-- Foreign banks can establish representative offices. No licence or special permission is required for this purpose.

-- The Parliament recently approved changes in policy which will allow foreign bank entry through subsidiaries only. The Government intends to follow a step-by-step strategy by initially allowing only a limited number of foreign bank subsidiaries. It is not yet clear when the change is going to take effect.

PORTUGAL
-- Entry of domestic and foreign private capital into the banking sector was prohibited by law in 1977 with the exception of regional development companies and parabanking institutions (e.g. investment and leasing companies). That prohibition was removed by Decree Law No. 406 of 19th November 1983.

SPAIN
-- The entry of foreign banking organisations in Spain is regulated by the provisions set forth in the Royal Decree 1388/1978 which allows the establishment of foreign banking presence in the forms of (i) representative offices; (ii) branches; and (iii) subsidiaries wholly-owned by non-resident institutions. The establishment of foreign banking organisations requires prior authorisation. For a representative office such an authorisation is granted by the Minister of the Economy on a proposal by the Bank of Spain after hearing the "Consejo Superior Bancario" (Banking Council). Branches and subsidiaries are authorised by the Council of Ministers on a proposal by the Minister of the Economy after hearing the Bank of Spain and the "Consejo Superior Bancario".

SWEDEN
-- According to Swedish banking law, foreign banks may not conduct business involving deposit and lending operations from establishments in Sweden (2). Foreign banks' establishments in Sweden are thus restricted to representative offices. Authorisation to establish such offices is subject to government approval.

-- In Sweden, there exist two kinds of non-bank financial institutions, i.e. credit companies and finance companies. Both must be joint stock companies under Swedish law. They may carry out various credit and financial operations in the same way as banks, but they may not collect deposits on account from the from the public. Credit companies as well as finance companies are subject to supervision by the Bank Inspection Board. Credit companies must be authorised by the Government. There are only a few of those; none of them with a foreign interest involved. A number of finance companies are wholly or partly owned by foreign subjects. These companies have been treated in the same way as those owned by Swedish nationals concerning establishment and market access. This also goes for domestic operations except regarding the possibility to acquire real property in Sweden or shares in a joint stock company under Swedish law that owns such property. In connection with the establishment of the committee to study the structure of the credit market, a bill was passed prohibiting non-residents from acquiring or establishing finance companies.

SWITZERLAND -- The establishment of a foreign banking organisation (representative office, branch, or subsidiary) is subject to prior authorisation by the Commission Fédérale des Banques.

-- Entry provisions apply equally to both domestic and foreign banks but in the latter case the following additional conditions must be met:

   i) Reciprocity applies with regard to the parent bank's country of origin;

   ii) The company's name must not give the impression that the bank is a Swiss one;

   iii) The National Bank receives the assurances necessary for the protection of Switzerland's credit and monetary policies.

TURKEY   -- The establishment of representative offices requires prior authorisation by the Foreign Investment Department. Applicants must submit a report containing an evaluation of the activities the office intends to engage in, the benefits expected from the representative office and its contribution to the host economy, as well as an account of the total amount of foreign currency required to meet general expenses, rents and wages.

-- The opening of branches and subsidiaries is subject to authorisation by the Council of Ministers. Foreign banks wishing to operate branches in Turkey must be joint-stock companies or have a corresponding legal status in the home country of the head office. The application for entry authorisation should include, inter alia, confirmation that the statute of the bank does not contain any provision contrary to the banking law of Turkey and that the bank has not been forbidden to engage in banking transactions or to accept deposits either in the home country or in any other country where it has branches.

UNITED   -- The opening of a representative office by a foreign
KINGDOM   bank is subject to notification to the Bank of England. The
                  . parent institution may be required to furnish certain
                     documentation.

                  -- Schedule 2 of the Banking Act 1979 sets out the minimum
                     criteria for authorisation of deposit-taking institutions,
                     including foreign banks' branches and subsidiaries. These
                     criteria are the same for both domestic and foreign-owned
                     institutions. However, under Section 3(5) of the Banking Act
                     of 1979, in the case of an institution whose principal place of
                     business is in a country or territory outside the United
                     Kingdom, the Bank may regard itself as satisfied that certain
                     of these criteria are fulfilled if the relevant supervisory
                     authorities in the country of origin inform the Bank that they
                     are satisfied with respect to the management of the institution
                     and its overall financial soundness and the Bank is satisfied
                     as to the nature and scope of the supervision exercised by
                     those authorities.

UNITED   -- Under the International Banking Act of 1978 (IBA), all
STATES   United States representative offices of foreign banks are
                     required to register with the Department of Treasury. There
                     are no restrictions or limitations on entry.

                  -- To establish an agency or a branch in the United States, a
                     foreign bank must apply either to the Comptroller of the
                     Currency for a Federal licence or to a particular state for a
                     state licence. Some states either (a) do not expressly permit
                     or (b) actually prohibit the establishment of state-licensed
                     agencies and branches by foreign banks. If a state does not
                     actually prohibit the establishment of such offices, the
                     Comptroller may license a Federal agency or branch in that
                     state, provided that the state is the foreign bank's "home
                     state" under the IBA. If the state is not the foreign bank's
                     home state, the Comptroller may license a Federal agency or
                     limited branch only if state law expressly permits
                     establishment of agencies or branches of foreign banks.

                  -- To establish a United States commercial bank, a foreign bank
                     must apply to the Federal Reserve Board under Section 3(a) of
                     the Bank Holding Company Act (BHCA). The Board considers the
                     same statutory criteria in acting on applications by foreign or
                     domestic parties to acquire or establish a United States bank.

                  -- Under the IBA, a foreign bank may establish an Edge Corporation
                     in any state with prior approval of the Board. (Edge
                     Corporations are chartered by the Board to engage in
                     international banking and financial operations and may be
                     established in locations outside the state in which their owner
                     operates.)

Table 1.2

RECIPROCITY PROVISIONS CONCERNING THE ESTABLISHMENT OF FOREIGN BANKING ORGANISATIONS (*)

AUSTRALIA -- Not applicable.

AUSTRIA -- None

BELGIUM -- None

CANADA -- The Minister of Finance must be satisfied that treatment as favourable for Canadian banks exists or will be arranged in the home jurisdiction of a foreign bank wishing to establish an operation in Canada.

DENMARK -- There are no specific legal provisions on reciprocity, but reciprocity considerations are taken into account when banks from non-EEC countries apply for entry in Denmark.

FINLAND -- No legal provisions but according to the Government Propositions to Parliament concerning foreign bank legislation, the principle of reciprocity is applicable to foreign banking presence in Finland.

FRANCE -- When considering an application for licence by a foreign bank, the Conseil National du Crédit takes into consideration the conditions applied to foreign bank entry in the applicant's home country.

GERMANY -- At present there are no reciprocity provisions. It is, however, being considered that such provisions be introduced with regard to branches of foreign banks.

GREECE -- None

IRELAND -- In considering an application by an overseas bank for a banking licence, the Central Bank would have regard to the attitude of the authorities of that bank's country of origin to possible applications by Irish banks to establish there. This however, would not be a determining factor.

ITALY -- Authorisation for the establishment of branches of outside-EEC banks is subject to the proviso that the principle of reciprocity is respected.

JAPAN -- Under specific circumstances, application of the reciprocity principle is required.

LUXEMBOURG -- None

---

* This Table summarises answers to item 1.2 of the questionnaire.

NETHERLANDS -- Section 7 of the Act on the Supervision of the Credit System empowers the Crown to determine grounds and directives, on the basis of which the Bank shall refuse to grant a licence, revoke a licence granted, or grant a licence subject to conditions in cases where institutions are concerned which have their registered office outside the EEC. This Section permits a policy of reciprocity to be conducted vis-à-vis countries where Netherlands banks meet with difficulties in setting up establishments. However, so far, no such directives have been issued.

NEW ZEALAND -- Not applicable.

NORWAY -- Not available.

PORTUGAL -- No reciprocity clause is explicitly embodied in the banking law.

SPAIN -- The authorisation for the establishment of foreign banks' branches or subsidiaries is granted according to criteria that take account of the reciprocity principle.

SWEDEN -- Not applicable.

SWITZERLAND -- The reciprocity principle is enshrined as a specific criteria in the Swiss banking law for granting authorisation to the establishment of foreign banking organisations.

TURKEY -- Reciprocity could be applied in terms of conditions required by the Council of Ministers at the stage of granting the authorisation for entry.

UNITED KINGDOM -- None

UNITED STATES -- There are no Federal reciprocity provisions but such provisions are applied to foreign banks' branches and agencies by some states.

Table 1.3

OTHER REQUIREMENTS, RESTRICTIONS AND IMPEDIMENTS AFFECTING FOREIGN BANK ENTRY (*)

AUSTRALIA -- Not applicable.

AUSTRIA -- None

BELGIUM -- All special licensing procedures apply equally to both foreign and domestic banking institutions. However, the authorisation to extend mortgage credits to be granted by the Ministry of Economic Affairs may be refused if reciprocity is not granted in the parent bank's country of origin.

-- Branches of foreign banks operating in Belgium are required to maintain a minimum "own capital" of at least BF 50 million (irrespective of the number of branches or offices of a foreign bank licensed to operate in Belgium). This amount is the same as for banks incorporated in Belgium. Since branches have no legal personality, special provisions concerning minimum capital have been established. Thus, the Banking Commission is empowered to determine what is regarded as "own capital" for this purpose. The "own capital" is defined as the endowment of the branch - i.e. the portion of the capital funds of the bank which has been permanently allocated to the branch for its activities in Belgium - plus any additions to it in the form of free reserves and accumulated profits that have been retained by the branch, to the extent that the aggregate of these two items corresponds to a net surplus of assets over liabilities in the Belgian balance sheet of the branch. The endowment must not be used to undertake operations outside Belgium and the Banking Commission requires proof that this endowment in no way corresponds to a liability of the parent bank to third parties. The Belgian balance sheet of the branch includes only assets and liabilities denominated in Belgian francs vis-à-vis Belgian residents.

-- A banking institution authorised to operate in Belgium must take the form of a "commercial company" with legal personality (Société Commerciale), which excludes the form of a one-man firm. This applies to both foreign and domestic institutions, it being understood that, in the case of branches, the parent institution must be a "commercial company".

-- There is no specific requirement on the nationality of personnel and management. However, non-residents are subject to the general provisions concerning foreigners working in Belgium (e.g. professional card or working permit).

---

* This Table summarises answers to items 1.3 to 1.8 of the questionnaire.

-- The Banking Commission requires a statement by the applicant that the opening of the branch or the subsidiary has been notified to the competent authorities of the home country and that the transfer of the required funds has been authorised. Moreover, in the case of branches, the applicant must provide a certified copy of the decision by the parent bank's management to earmark a portion of the bank's capital to the branch set up in Belgium.

CANADA
-- Once the Governor in Council has approved the commencement of business in Canada, foreign bank subsidiaries are required to obtain a licence subject to terms and conditions issued by the Minister of Finance. Initial licences are for periods specified in the licence but not longer than one year and renewal licences are for a period of up to three years.

-- Foreign banks wishing to incorporate subsidiaries in Canada should be known as a bank by the regulatory authorities in its home jurisdiction and should generally be in the business of lending and borrowing money, with the latter including the acceptance of deposits transferable by order. It is desirable that the foreign bank be widely-held, i.e. where no one shareholder (and those associated with him) effectively controls the bank. Exceptions are made if the bank is owned or controlled by a foreign government.

-- One half of the Board of Directors of a foreign bank subsidiary must be Canadian citizens ordinarily resident in Canada. Three-quarters of the directors of any other bank must meet those criteria.

-- A letter of comfort authorised by the Board of Directors of the foreign bank must accompany the application for the establishment of a foreign bank subsidiary.

DENMARK
-- Branches of foreign banks must have a registered paid-up capital (branch capital) of at least DKr 25 million, i.e. the minimum capital requirement for Danish banks. The branch capital requirement applies only to the first branch set up by a foreign bank. The own-capital of a branch comprises the registered branch capital plus/minus any accumulated profits/losses in the branch and less the net debt due to the branch by the parent company or other companies belonging to the same concern. The own-capital must not fall below the registered capital.

-- A bank cannot, without permission, hold more than 30 per cent of the share-capital of another bank.

-- Members of the Board of Directors and Managing Directors must have a permanent address in Denmark (this does not apply to EEC-citizens) and must comply with certain requirements of qualifications and of an ethical nature.

FINLAND
-- With the permission of the Ministry of Finance, a foreigner is

entitled to acquire shares in Finnish commercial banks, mortgage banks and credit companies. Total share ownership by foreigners must not exceed 20 per cent of the share capital. A foreigner is defined as a person who is not a Finnish citizen, a foreign company, partnership, association and other organisation, foundation or institution. The Council of State (the Government) may, for particular reasons, grant a foreign credit institution the right to acquire more than 20 per cent of the shares. A credit institution is defined as a bank or other joint-stock or limited liability enterprise that is primarily engaged in the business of borrowing, lending or the mediating of loans, or that handles monetary transactions.

-- According to the banking legislation, the members of the Board of Directors and the Supervisory Board and the General Manager must be unimpeachable and legally competent Finnish citizens residing in Finland, unless the Ministry of Finance grants dispensation from the requirements on residence and nationality. The auditors of a Finnish bank shall also be Finnish citizens residing in Finland, unless the Ministry of Finance grants dispensation. The majority of the auditors of the bank shall be Finnish citizens residing in Finland. The Ministry of Finance has made a decision in principle that half of the members of the Board of Directors and the Supervisory Board may be foreigners or Finnish citizens residing abroad. The General Manager is allowed to be a foreigner or a Finnish citizen residing abroad.

-- When a foreign bank or credit institution applies for permission to establish a wholly-owned or majority-owned banking subsidiary, the applicant is expected to provide a letter of comfort or a guarantee for the subsidiary.

FRANCE   -- Branches of foreign banks must maintain an endowment capital at least equal to the minimum capital required for companies incorporated under French law.

-- The owners of the capital should have adequate banking experience. If this condition is not fulfilled, a significant part of the capital is to be entrusted to a bank of good standing which should participate in the management of the bank.

-- In principle, management of the bank is confined to citizens of EEC states. However, derogations to this rule are applied in a liberal fashion by the Ministry of Finance.

-- There is no general requirement concerning guarantees and "comfort letters" from parent institutions. However, the Commission de Contrôle des Banques may require that a blocked account in French francs be opened by the parent bank with a view to guaranteeing the branch's liabilities. This requirement has been applied very rarely.

GERMANY   -- Branches of foreign banks must have separate own funds; their liable capital is deemed to be the working capital supplied to them by their foreign parent institutions and operating profits retained to enlarge their capital and reserves, less the amount of a credit balance on inter-branch settlement accounts.

-- There are no provisions on nationality of personnel and management. Managers of branches of foreign banks or of foreign-owned subsidiaries are required to have a reasonable command of the German language, such as is necessary to direct a banking institution in Germany. As for competence, they are subject to the same regulations as managers of German banks: they must have the professional qualifications necessary for managing the bank or branch. According to Section 33 of the Banking Act, a person shall normally be assumed to have the professional qualifications necessary for managing a bank if three years' managing experience in a bank of comparable size and type is proved. Foreign bank managers, in addition, must show proof of a one-year banking activity in the Federal Republic of Germany.

GREECE

-- For the total of their branches in Greece, foreign banks must import and convert into drachmae the foreign exchange equivalent of Dr 1 billion, which represents endowment capital for their operations in Greece. The requirement applies to banks expanding their branch network after January 1981. For foreign banks established in Greece prior to January 1981 and not expanding their network after that date, there are in most cases requirements for importation of specific foreign exchange amounts per branch, which were set as pre-conditions for granting the specific entry licence.

-- The majority of the members of the Board of Directors of any bank established in Greece must be of Greek nationality. Senior officials must be resident in Greece. Foreign nationals must obtain work permits and a quota system applies to foreign nationals per bank.

-- There is no general rule with regard to guarantees and "letters of comfort" from parent institutions. In examining applications, the monetary authorities may stipulate specific requirements.

IRELAND

-- Endowment capital requirements applying to branches of foreign banks are similar to the capital requirements for other licensed banking institutions.

-- The Central Bank must be satisfied that the beneficial ownership and capital structure of a licence holder are such as best to ensure:

   i) The capacity of the licence holder to be independent of dominant personal and commercial interests;

   ii) Cohesion in the manner in which the business of the licence holder is directed by its owners;

51

iii) A capacity to provide such new capital for the licence holder as may be required in the future;

iv) A willingness and capacity on the part of the licence holder to comply with the Central Bank's licensing and supervision requirements and standards.

-- A majority of the Board of Directors of licence holders incorporated in Ireland may be required to be Irish or nationals of other Member States of the EEC. Banks established in Ireland on a branch basis shall have a local Supervisory Board and the majority of the members of the Board may be required to be Irish or nationals of other Member States of the EEC. In practice, the Central Bank does not insist on strict compliance with the nationality requirements.

-- The business of a licence holder and the management of the day-to-day operations of its offices in Ireland shall be directed by at least two persons, who shall be resident in Ireland. The Central Bank must be satisfied in regard to the suitability of the management structure of a licensed bank and that there is adequate provision for suitable management succession. In particular, it must be satisfied (a) that executive directors, or executive members of local supervisory boards in the case of branches of externally-owned banks, and senior management executives are persons of integrity and have suitable experience in banking, and (b) that non-executive directors, or non-executive members of local supervisory boards in the case of branches of externally-owned banks, are persons of integrity and have suitable experience in banking, industry or commerce.

-- The Central Bank requires that the liabilities of a licensed bank which is a subsidiary company shall be guaranteed to the satisfaction of the Bank by the parent company. In this regard, a "letter of comfort" is sought from the parent company.

ITALY   -- The minimum capital required for the opening of the first branch of a foreign bank is L 15 billion at present.

-- Branches of foreign banks are required to provide "comfort letters" from their parent institutions. Such a letter is not compulsory in the case of EEC banks, though failure to produce one results in a branch's operational limits being severely curtailed.

-- In some regions with special statutes, local legislation gives the region autonomous powers in credit matters with regard to the establishment of new banks and the opening of branches.

JAPAN   -- None

LUXEMBOURG   -- Branches of foreign banks are required to have a minimum capital of LF 250 million.

-- Directors of a bank, either foreign or domestic, must satisfy the requirement of respectability and professional qualification.

NETHERLANDS -- Enterprises and institutions have to keep separate accounts for their business conducted in the Netherlands. The "own resources" of establishments in the Netherlands of enterprises or institutions which have their registered office outside the Netherlands are given by the amount of capital and free reserves that is shown in these separate accounts, less the debit balances in the name of the parent institution, insofar as these debit balances exceed the funds invested with the enterprise or institution by its Netherlands establishment for account and risk of third parties. The establishment shall employ in the Netherlands a sum corresponding at least to its own resources.

-- Anyone who, by virtue of shares or partnership rights held directly or indirectly in a credit institution, is able to cast -- (or have cast on his behalf) -- more than one-twentieth of the number of votes in the general meeting of shareholders or the meeting of partners respectively, or is otherwise able to exercise (or have exercised on his behalf) a comparable degree of direct or indirect control in a credit institution, shall not be allowed to cast (or have cast on his behalf) one or more votes or to exercise otherwise (or have otherwise exercised on his behalf) a comparable degree of control until a declaration of no-objection has been obtained. Such a declaration shall be granted unless the Bank is of the opinion that it is contrary to sound banking policy or could lead to an undesirable development of the credit system, or unless the Minister of Finance is of the opinion that it could lead to an undesirable development of the credit system. In practice, an important element of this policy is the countering of the intermingling of banking and insurance activities which could lead to undue concentrations of economic power in the Netherlands. No distinction is made between foreign and domestic institutions.

-- There are no regulatory and administrative provisions on nationality and language requirements of personnel and management. As for the competence of the management, the Bank may raise objections to one or more persons who determine the (day-to-day) policy of a credit institution, if it considers that, in view of inadequate expertise or past history, it is to be feared that the interests of the creditors might be at risk. The Bank will generally judge the expertise on the basis of education and training received and practical experience gained. Past history may be judged by asking for references.

NEW ZEALAND -- Not applicable.

NORWAY -- Not available.

PORTUGAL -- Decree Law No. 406 of 19th November 1983 removed the prohibition, in force since 1977, on the entry and establishment of foreign banks in Portugal. However, the new regulations governing foreign banks with respect to minimum capital, limitations of individual shareholders participation in the share capital etc. have not yet been published.

SPAIN   -- The earmarked capital for a branch of a foreign bank is set a minimum of Ptas 2 billion payable in foreign currency or convertible pesetas, of which half is disbursed upon opening and the remainder within one year.

            -- The capital for a subsidiary of a foreign bank is in Ptas 2 billion payable in foreign currency or convertible pesetas of which half is disbursed upon opening and the remainder within two years. In addition, bank subsidiaries must have an initial reserve of Ptas 2 billion, fully disbursed.

            -- Spanish corporate law requires a minimum of three partners to register a limited company. Along this requirement, the Royal Decree 1388/1978 sets as a provision that the capital of a subsidiary can only be subscribed by banks. Therefore three banks are needed to establish a subsidiary, although if control has to be exercised by only one of them, the remaining two need only subscribe a minimum number - one - of shares.

            -- The Royal Decree of 1388/1978 does not set any requirements of guarantees and "letters of comfort" from parent institutions although in some special cases the authorities have in fact requested "letters of comfort". In the case of branches, the opening must be under the trade name and full responsibility of the parent.

SWEDEN   -- Not applicable.

SWITZERLAND -- A branch of a foreign bank is required to have an endowment capital of at least SF 2 million which must be transferred in Switzerland.

            -- As a general rule, for an company domiciled in Switzerland the majority of the Board of Directors must have Swiss nationality and residence. Working permits for foreigners are subject to quotas.

            -- The Commission Fédérale des Banques may ask guarantees for agencies of a foreign bank.

TURKEY   -- A bank authorised to operate a branch in Turkey must transfer to Turkey the amount of capital indicated in the admission decree as well as reserve funds, if any. The foreign exchange brought as capital and reserves must be converted into Turkish Liras at the Central Bank and blocked therein until the actual opening of the branch. Requirements for the earmarked capital applying to the branches of foreign banks have been determined in through the admission decrees since 1981 as follows:

a) For the opening of the first branch the earmarked capital should not be less than $6 million, or equivalent in convertible foreign currency;

b) For additional branches, the required capital should not be less than $3 million, or equivalent in convertible foreign currency.

-- Foreign banks operating through a branch in Turkey must obtain an authorisation from the Under-Secretariat of Treasury and Foreign Trade for opening any additional branch. Banks operating more than one branch in Turkey must submit a statement to the Ministry of Finance indicating which branch should be regarded as the main office in Turkey.

-- Foreign banks should use Turkish language in their activities and transactions in Turkey.

-- Guarantees and letters of comfort could be required if deemed necessary.

UNITED
KINGDOM

-- A branch of a foreign bank is not regarded as a separate entity, but rather as an integral part of the total operation of the bank worldwide. Accordingly, it is felt inappropriate to expect branches to maintain their own capital. Branches are, however, expected to maintain adequate liquidity and keep within agreed foreign currency exposure guidelines. The Bank regards the supervisors in the country of origin as having the primary responsibility for supervision of these banks including their branches in the United Kingdom. Indeed the Bank obtains from these overseas supervisors an assurance that they supervise the bank on such a basis. Confirmation is also sought that in the opinion of the overseas supervisors the bank is prudently run and that its capital adequacy and liquidity are satisfactory. While regular contact between the Bank and foreign branches is maintained, reporting requirements are less extensive and prudential meetings normally less frequent than for United Kingdom incorporated institutions.

-- There are no specific restrictions on ownership of a bank under the Banking Act. However, under Schedule 2 of the Act, the Bank of England must be satisfied that at least two individuals effectively direct the business of an authorised institution. The Bank believes that it is not desirable for a bank's fortunes to be tied too closely to an individual or commercial entity and bears this consideration in mind when it is consulted about changes in ownership and control.

-- There are no provisions relating to nationality imposed by the Bank but any person resident in the United Kingdom who is not a national of a Member State of the EEC must obtain a work permit from the Department of Employment. However, the Bank of England expects those involved in senior management and in day-to-day market operations to have adequate knowledge of English. As regards the competence of management, the Bank must be satisfied that all directors, controllers and managers of a licensed institution are fit and proper persons to hold those positions and that, in the case of a recognised bank, the business will be carried on with integrity and prudence and with those professional skills which are consistent with the scale and range of the institutions's activities. In the case of a foreign bank, under certain circumstances it may be required that at least one member of senior management has appropriate experience in the London market, and this would be a pre-requisite for any individual appointed as senior foreign currency dealer.

-- It is the bank's policy to obtain from parent institutions outside the United Kingdom a letter of comfort which may be seen as a formal acknowledgement of the moral commitment to support a United Kingdom deposit-taking subsidiary.

UNITED
STATES

-- Generally, there are no impediments to a foreign bank's United States operations that result from its foreign status. Moreover, in order to take into account the fact that in many countries abroad separation between banking and commerce is not required, as it is in the United States, foreign banks are exempt from certain prohibitions that apply to domestic companies regarding the extent to which banks may engage in non-banking activities in the United States.

-- Under the International Banking Act, there is a statutory requirement for a 5 per cent asset pledge for Federally licensed branches of foreign banks. Some states have similar asset pledge requirements for state-licensed branches of foreign banks.

-- In general, non-banking organisations, foreign or domestic, may not own banks in the United States.

-- In approving application under the Bank Holding Company Act, the Federal Reserve Board is required to assess the managerial resources of an applicant. The IBA permits up to one-half of the directors of national banks to be foreign nationals. State law may or may not require that directors be United States citizens. There is no requirement to employ United States nationals. Foreign banks are subject to Federal and state laws in the United States providing for non-discriminatory treatment in such areas as employment and extension of credit. Reports for regulatory and statistical purposes must be submitted in English.

-- There are no formal requirements for guarantees and "letters of comfort" from parent institutions. However, it is Board policy - and the Board has issued a policy statement to that effect - that foreign banks are expected to be a source of strength to their United States operations.

-- Some states, such as New York, require that a bank chartered in the state be able to establish some form of banking office in a foreign bank's home country in order to operate a branch in New York. Also, some states do not permit foreign banks to establish branches.

Table 2.1

REGULATIONS RESTRICTING FOREIGN ACQUISITIONS
OF PARTICIPATIONS IN INDIGENOUS BANKS (*)

AUSTRALIA   -- It has been longstanding Australian Government policy not to allow foreign interests to acquire participations, other than of a small portfolio nature, in existing Australian banks.

          -- Under current government foreign investment policy, proposals by foreign banks to acquire, or to increase, a substantial interest in an existing non-bank financial intermediary are closely examined by the Foreign Investment Review Board which makes recommendations to the Treasurer. Current policy provides that such proposals must show substantial net economic benefits to Australia or, where the economic benefits are small, must involve an effective partnership between Australian interests and the foreign investors in the ownership and control of the company concerned.

AUSTRIA   -- Provisions concerning the acquisition of participations in Austrian banks apply equally to both foreign or domestic investors. To acquire ownership of a bank, a licence is required (Act. 8 of the Austrian Banking Law).

BELGIUM   -- Non-resident acquisition of participations in Belgian banks is subject to two general provisions applying to any foreign investment in Belgian companies:

             i) Authorisation by the Minister of Finance is required for any takeover bid on public companies by residents of countries outside the EEC;

            ii) The Minister of Economic Affairs, the Minister of Finance and the State Secretary to the regional economy must receive prior notification of any operations leading to the acquisition of at least one third of the capital of enterprises operating in Belgium and whose capital is of at least BF 100 million.

          -- Any merger in the banking sector must be authorised by the Banking Commission. This provision applies equally to the acquisition of majority participations. In the context of the protocol on the autonomy of the banking function, any significant change in the relative share, the ownership or control of shareholders' participations is subject to prior consultation with the Banking Commission. These provisions apply equally to both Belgian and foreign shareholders.

_____

*   This Table summarises answers to items 2.1 and 2.2 of the questionnaire.

CANADA -- No one shareholder or group of associated shareholders are permitted to own directly, or indirectly, more than 10 per cent of shares of a bank and the basic limit on shares held by non-residents for Schedule A banks (banks whose shares are widely-held) is 25 per cent. Exceptions are made for Schedule B banks, including subsidiaries of foreign banks, and grandfathered Schedule A banks.

DENMARK -- Participations are limited by foreign-exchange regulations and by the provision that a bank cannot without permission hold more than 30 per cent of the share capital of another bank. This latter provision applies equally to domestic and foreign banks.

FINLAND -- Foreign banks and other credit institutions are allowed to acquire shares in Finnish commercial and mortage banks or credit companies. A foreigner or a foreign bank may not participate in the election of trustees of a Finnish savings bank nor become a member of a Finnish co-operative bank.

-- With the permission of the Ministry of Finance, a foreigner is entitled to acquire shares in a Finnish commercial bank, a mortgage bank or a credit company; total share ownership by foreigners must not exceed 20 per cent of the share capital. The Council of State (the Government) may for particular reasons grant a foreign credit institution the right to acquire more than 20 per cent of the shares. A permission by the Bank of Finland for receiving investment funds from abroad for share capital is also needed.

FRANCE -- There is no specific regulation concerning the acquisition of participations by non-residents in indigenous banks which is, however, subject to exchange control provisions. Within specific limits, any change in the ownership structure of a bank incorporated in France requires prior authorisation by the Conseil National du Crédit.

GERMANY -- None

GREECE -- Non-resident participation is not usually allowed to exceed 40 per cent of the capital stock of a bank established in Greece. Exceptions to this practice were authorised in a few cases (up to 51 per cent).

IRELAND -- Proposals by foreign banks to acquire participations in indigenous banks are treated in the same way as domestic proposals.

ITALY -- In view of the legal constraints in force and of the public nature of the majority of banks, the question of the acquisition of participations only concerns in practice the banks set up as joint-stock companies (i.e. the ordinary credit banks). In their case the sale of all or a part of the capital to foreigners is not subject to authorisation by the supervisory authorities (except as regards compliance with the foreign currency regulations), the decision falling within the sphere of banks' autonomous powers. With regard to the "banks of national interest", their shares can only be held by Italian citizens and residents of EEC countries.

JAPAN   -- According to the Anti-Monopoly Law, authorisation by the Fair Trade Commission is required for the acquisition of over 5 per cent of the equity of another company by a financial institution, foreign or domestic.

LUXEMBOURG   -- None

NETHERLANDS -- None

NEW ZEALAND -- Aquisitions or participations in New Zealand incorporated banks would be subject to the overseas investment regulations of 1974. Consent would be required where a 25 per cent or more equity participation was sought by an overseas person. Three of the four trading banks operating in New Zealand would be subject to the regulations. However, as the Bank of New Zealand is wholly government owned and there is no intention at present to change its status, the regulation of foreign acquisitions in this case is not a question. The ANZ which is New Zealand incorporated is 25 per cent New Zealand owned. If the Australian parent company wished to increase its holdings or to dispose of 25 per cent or more of the ANZ's shares to another foreign party, consent would be required under the overseas investment regulations. The National Bank is wholly owned by Lloyds is also incorporated in New Zealand. The acquisition of 25 per cent or more of its shares by a foreign person would therefore also require consent under the regulations. The fourth trading bank, Westpac, operates as a branch of an Australian bank. A change in ownership of this branch would not be subject to the regulations.

NORWAY   -- Foreigners can, without a licence, acquire up to a total of 10 per cent, and with permission from the Government up to 25 per cent, of the share capital in Norwegian banks.

PORTUGAL   -- The acquisition of interests in Portugal was forbidden by law in 1977, but foreign participation was permitted in parabanking institutions (e.g. investment and leasing companies) and in regional development companies. That prohibition was eliminated by Decree Law No. 406 of 19th November 1983.

SPAIN   -- Foreign control participation in indigenous banks requires prior authorisation by the Minister of Economy and Finance. However, these authorisations have been granted only exceptionally.

SWEDEN   -- Foreign acquisition or participation in Swedish banks is not permitted.

-- There are no special restrictions on the nationality of credit companies. In 1983, a bill was passed prohibiting non-residents from acquiring or establishing finance companies.

SWITZERLAND -- The acquisition of majority participations in Swiss banks is subject to prior authorisation. The criteria applied for authorisation are the same as for the entry and establishment of a foreign bank subsidiary (reciprocity, the company's name must not give the impression that the bank is a Swiss one, and adherence to the National Bank's credit and monetary policy).

TURKEY -- Foreign acquisition of participations in indigenous banks is regulated according to the provisions of the Decree on the Framework of Foreign Capital under the law concerning the Encouragement of Foreign Capital. Upon completion by the Undersecretariat of Treasury and Foreign Trade and by the Ministry of Industry and Commerce of a study of the application, the relevant decree for authorisation is submitted to the Council of Ministers. Foreign participation may not represent less than 10 per cent and more than 49 per cent of the bank's capital.

UNITED KINGDOM -- There are no formal restrictions on the acquisition of less than 15 per cent of the share capital of a recognised bank or licensed deposit-taker. The acquisition of a participation of more than 15 per cent of the capital of a bank whether by domestic or foreign interests falls within the ambit of a notice issued by the Bank of England on 16th November 1972. This requires that the Bank be consulted on all such proposals as early as possible and before any formal negotiations are undertaken. A flexible approach is maintained but, in general, approval for the acquisition will be subject to agreement between the parties concerned and to the satisfaction of tests relating to capital, management, reputation and future intentions.

UNITED STATES - To acquire a United States commercial bank, a foreign bank must apply to the Federal Reserve Board under Section 3(a) of the Bank Holding Company Act (BHCA). The Board considers the same statutory criteria in acting on applications by foreign or domestic parties to acquire or establish a United States bank. It should be noted, however, that under the BHCA, up to 5 per cent of the voting shares of a bank may be acquired by any organisation without prior approval by Federal banking agencies, while acquisition of a larger proportion may require approval by a Federal agency. Specifically, acquisition of more than 5 per cent but less than 25 per cent of a bank might require Federal regulatory approval, while acquisitions of 25 per cent or more always requires Federal regulatory approval.

Table 2.2

OTHER PROVISIONS APPLYING TO FOREIGN ACQUISITION
OF INDIGENOUS BANKS (*)

AUSTRALIA -- Not applicable.

AUSTRIA -- None

BELGIUM -- None

CANADA -- Responsibility for competition policy in the banking sector is shared between the Minister of Consumer and Corporate Affairs and the Minister of Finance. The Minister of Finance, under the provisions of the Bank Act has authority to approve bank mergers which he certifies as being in the public interest and which are necessary for the stability of the financial system.

-- Restrictions on who can own a bank:

   i) Her Majesty in right of Canada is not permitted to own shares of a bank;

   ii) No one person or group of associated persons may own or control more than 10 per cent of the shares of a bank. Exceptions are made for new banks and subsidiaries of foreign banks;

   iii) Provincial governments may own up to 25 per cent of the shares of a new bank for 10 years and 10 per cent thereafter;

   iv) Financial corporations may own up to 25 per cent of the shares of a new bank for ten years.

-- Shares of a bank may not be transferred to foreign governments or their agents except in the special case where the parent bank of a foreign bank subsidiary is a state-owned bank.

DENMARK -- Mergers and amalgamations require authorisation by the Minister of Industry. Provisions apply equally to both foreign and Danish banks.

-- A bank cannot without permission hold more than 30 per cent of the share capital of another bank.

-- Members of the Board of Directors and Managing Directors must have a permanent address in Denmark (this does not apply to EEC citizens) and must comply with certain requirements of qualification and of an ethical nature.

---

* This Table summarises answers to items 2.2 to 2.8 of the questionnaire.

FINLAND   -- According to the banking legislation, the members of the Board
              of Directors and the Supervisory Board and the Central Manager
              must be unimpeachable and legally competent Finnish citizens
              residing in Finland unless the Ministry of Finance grants
              dispensation from the requirements on residence and
              nationality. The auditors of a Finnish bank shall also be
              Finnish citizens residing in Finland, unless the Ministry of
              Finance grants dispensation. The majority of the auditors of
              the bank shall be Finnish citizens residing in Finland. The
              Ministry of Finance has made a decision in principle that half
              of the members of the Boards of Directors and the Supervisory
              Board may be foreigners or Finnish citizens residing abroad.
              The General Manager is allowed to be a foreigner or a Finnish
              citizen resident abroad.

           -- When a foreign bank or credit institution applies for a
              permission to own less than 20 per cent of the total share
              capital, it is not necessary to provide a letter of comfort of
              a guarantee with regard to the foreign investment. If the
              total foreign investment is more than 50 per cent of the share
              capital of the indigenous bank, the foreign applicant(s) is/are
              expected to provide a letter of comfort as a guarantee.

FRANCE   -- The criteria applied for the licensing of a bank with foreign
              interests are the same as for the establishment of a foreign
              bank subsidiary (see Tables 1.2 and 1.3).

GERMANY   -- The general provisions of the German Anti-Trust Act apply to
              mergers in the banking sector. According to this Act, mergers
              of a certain magnitude have to be reported to the Federal
              Anti-Trust Authority; they may be forbidden if the
              conglomeration resulting from the merger would gain a dominant
              market position and thus endanger competition.

GREECE   -- The majority of the members of the Board of Directors of a bank
              established in Greece must be of Greek nationality.

           -- In examining applications, the monetary authorities may require
              specific guarantees from the investing institution.

IRELAND   -- The same requirements apply as for the establishment of a
              foreign bank subsidiary (see Tables 1.2 and 1.3).

ITALY   -- Mergers of banks are subject to prior authorisation by the Bank
              of Italy.

JAPAN   -- Mergers among banks in Japan, both foreign and domestic, are
              possible, subject to the approval of the Minister of Finance
              (Act. 30-31 of the Banking Laws).

LUXEMBOURG -- None

NETHERLANDS -- Mergers in the banking sector are not allowed unless a
              declaration of no-objection is obtained. Such a declaration
              shall be granted unless the merger could contravene sound

banking policy or could lead to an undesirable development of the credit system.

-- Anyone who, by virtue of shares of partnership rights held directly or indirectly in a credit institution, is able to cast (or have cast on his behalf) more than one-twentieth of the number of votes in the general meeting of shareholders or the meeting of partners respectively, or is otherwise able to exercise (or have exercised on his behalf) a comparable degree of direct or indirect control in a credit institution, shall not be allowed to cast (or have cast on his behalf) one or more votes or to exercise otherwise (or have otherwise exercised on his behalf) a comparable degree of control until a declaration of no-objection has been obtained. Such a declaration shall be granted unless the Bank is of the opinion that it is contrary to sound banking policy or could lead to an undesirable development of the credit system. In practice, an important element of this policy is the countering of the intermingling of banking and insurance activities which could lead to undue concentrations of economic power in the Netherlands. No distinction is made between foreign and domestic institutions.

NEW ZEALAND -- Not applicable.

NORWAY -- Not applicable.

PORTUGAL -- The Decree Law No. 406 of 19th November 1983 removed the prohibition, in force since 1977, on the entry and establishment of foreign banks in Portugal. However, regulatory measures accompanying this law have not yet been published.

SPAIN -- Participations by foreigners in newly-created domestic banks are restricted to individuals during the first five years of life. See also Spanish entry in Table 2.1.

-- Letters of comfort must be provided in the case of foreign participations in indigenous banks if the foreign institution acquires a controlling interest.

SWEDEN -- Not applicable.

SWITZERLAND -- None

TURKEY -- The granting of authorisation for foreign participation in indigenous banks is subject to reciprocity considerations.

-- Guarantees may be required by the investing bank.

UNITED KINGDOM (3) -- Mergers between banks, as between other companies, are subject to the provisions of the Fair Trading Act 1973 which empowers the Secretary of State to refer a proposed merger to the Monopolies and Mergers Commission to assess whether the proposal is likely to restrain competition or is otherwise against the public interest.

-- There are no specific restrictions on ownership of a bank under the Banking Act. However, under Schedule 2 of the Act the Bank of England must be satisfied that at least two individuals effectively direct the business of an authorised institution. The Bank believes that it is not desirable for a bank's fortunes to be tied too closely to an individual or commmercial entity and bears this consideration in mind when it is consulted about changes in ownership and control.

-- There are no restrictions on the nationality of directors but any person resident in the United Kingdom who is not a national of a Member state of the EEC must obtain a work permit from the Department of Employment. However, the Bank of England expects those involved in senior management and in day-to-day market operations to have adequate knowledge of English. As regards the competence of management, the Bank must be satisfied that all directors, controllers and managers of a licensed institution are fit and proper persons to hold those positions and that, in the case of a recognised bank, the business will be carried on with integrity and prudence and with those professional skills which are consistent with the scale and range of the institution's activities.

-- It is the Bank's policy to obtain from parent institutions outside the United Kingdom a letter of comfort which may be seen as a formal acknowledgement of the moral commitment to support a United Kingdom deposit-taking subsidiary.

UNITED   -- None
STATES

Part II

OPERATIONS OF ESTABLISHED FOREIGN-OWNED
BANKING ORGANISATIONS

Table 3.1

LIMITATIONS ON THE EXPANSION OF FOREIGN BRANCH NETWORKS (*)

AUSTRALIA -- The banking authorities held by BNP and BNZSB are conditional in that they specify the points at which the respective banks may carry on banking business; the approval of the Treasurer (a Government Minister) is required for those banks to establish additional points of representation. In this regard they differ from the authorities held by the indigenous banks and BNZ.

AUSTRIA -- Occasionally the licence is granted only on the stipulation that no branches shall be established. This applies also to new domestic banks.

BELGIUM -- Not applicable.

CANADA -- Closely-held banks, including subsidiaries of foreign banks, may not open any branch outside Canada but they are permitted to establish one branch in addition to their head office in Canada. Additional branches may be opened subject to the approval of the Minister of Finance. In practice, branches are not restricted but are encouraged. However, it is desirable to have a regional distribution of branches. The matter of branches is also important for purposes of reciprocity.

DENMARK -- Same as for Danish banks.

FINLAND -- The Articles of Association of established foreign-owned banking subsidiaries which, like those of domestically-owned banks, must be confirmed by the Ministry of Finance do not provide for the establishment of branches in Finland.

FRANCE -- Same as for French banks.

GERMANY -- Same as for German banks.

GREECE -- Same as for Greek banks.

IRELAND -- Same as for Irish banks.

---

*   This Table summarises answers to item 3.1 of the questionnaire.

ITALY   -- Same as for Italian banks.

JAPAN   -- Same as for Japanese banks.

LUXEMBOURG   -- Same as for Luxembourg banks.

NETHERLANDS   -- Same as for Dutch banks.

NEW ZEALAND   -- Same as for New Zealand banks.

NORWAY   -- Not applicable.

PORTUGAL   -- Same as for Portuguese banks.

SPAIN   -- Foreign banks established under the provision of the Royal
                    Decree 1388/1978 are limited as to the number of branches that
                    they can open. Presently that number is three. For a
                    subsidiary of a foreign bank the number of branches will thus
                    be two, in addition to the head office.

SWEDEN   -- Not applicable.

SWITZERLAND   -- Same as for Swiss banks.

TURKEY   -- According to the resolution of the related authorities, the
                    maximum number of branches which a foreign bank can open in
                    Turkey should be five. Only one branch can be opened in a
                    city. Exceptionally two branches can be opened in Istanbul,
                    the one on the Anatolian side, the other one on the European
                    side.

UNITED   -- Same as for United Kingdom banks.
KINGDOM

UNITED   -- Virtually all United States banks may operate branch offices
STATES   only in their principal state of operation. Foreign banks may,
                    however, operate agencies and branches in more than one state
                    subject to the provisions discussed below. The International
                    Banking Act (IBA) established a policy of national treatment
                    for foreign banks and attempted to foster competitive equity
                    between domestic and foreign banks in the United States by
                    limiting interstate expansion of domestic deposit-taking
                    capabilities of foreign banks. Under the IBA, a foreign bank
                    with domestic deposit-taking offices in more than one state
                    must select one of those states as its "home state". The
                    foreign bank may continue to establish agencies or branches
                    outside its home state, but such branches must agree to accept
                    only deposits that may be accepted by an Edge Corporation.
                    Within the home state, the foreign bank may establish
                    additional domestic deposit-taking offices if the state
                    permits. The IBA places no limits on the deposit-taking
                    activities of offices that existed or had been applied for on
                    or before 27th July 1978, nor on the lending powers of agencies
                    and branches outside the home state.

-- A United States bank holding company is prohibited from acquiring a bank outside its principal state of operation unless specifically permitted by state law. Similar treatment applies to foreign banks. A foreign bank that has no subsidiary bank in the United States (and, therefore, is not a bank holding company under the Bank Holding Company Act - BHCA) is precluded by the IBA from acquiring a bank outside its home state. A foreign bank that is already a bank holding company continues to be limited by the provisions of the BHCA that preclude the acquisition of a bank in a state other than that in which its subsidiary bank is located.

Table 3.2

DIFFERENTIAL RESTRICTIONS ON THE TYPE OF SERVICES THAT CAN BE OFFERED AND ON THE RANGE OF ACTIVITIES IN WHICH FOREIGN BANKS CAN ENGAGE (*)

AUSTRALIA   -- None

AUSTRIA   -- In general practice, the licence for a new domestic bank or a foreign banking institution excludes taking savings deposits. After a certain time, however, this type of business is permitted.

-- There is no impediment in principle to access to government and other public authorities' deposits, but such business is not usual.

-- Normally the licence excludes management of, and participation in, securities issues. Issuance of bonds by banks is normally not permitted under the licence.

-- Acquisition of equity participation of a permanent nature in Austrian banks is subject to the acquisition of a licence according to Article 8 of the Banking Law.

BELGIUM   -- None

CANADA   -- No individual restrictions apply to lending to domestic residents. According to the Inspector General's ruling, no more than 50 per cent of Canadian dollar assets can be funded offshore.

-- Foreign bank subsidiaries have unrestricted access to the Canadian commercial money market. However, foreign banks are not permitted to guarantee the money market paper of affiliates in Canada, except issues of foreign bank subsidiaries and non-bank affiliates which have been approved by the Minister of Finance.

-- A foreign bank that owns a foreign bank subsidiary is generally restricted in Canada to that investment and the resultant investment powers under the Bank Act pertaining to the foreign bank subsidiary. Canadian banks are precluded from taking large equity positions in non-financial corporations. Foreign banks may hold, however, other Canadian bank shares held on 23rd October 1979 and up to 10 per cent of the voting stock of other Canadian corporations. Further, there are exceptions with respect to foreign bank holding of Canadian corporations of a non-financial nature.

---

*   This Table summarises answers to item 3.2 of the questionnaire.

-- For those foreign banks that operate in Canada through non-bank affiliates, rather than through foreign bank subsidiaries, particular restrictions apply with regard to the solicitation of deposits from the public. The non-bank affiliate may not engage in both lending money and accepting deposits transferable by order. In addition, the non-bank affiliate must, when borrowing funds, refrain from using the guarantee of the foreign bank unless it has the permission of the Minister of Finance.

DENMARK   -- None

FINLAND   -- Foreign-owned banks must obtain the permission of the Bank of Finland before acquiring an equity stake in a domestic financial or non-financial enterprise. No similar provision applies to domestically-owned banks, but the right of commercial banks, whether domestically- or foreign-owned, to own shares in both financial and non-financial enterprises is restricted.

FRANCE   -- There is no regulation applying differentially to domestic and foreign-owned banks. However, it is an established practice that the lead manager of bond issues denominated in French francs should be a member of the "Comité des Emissions" which includes a small number of banks.

GERMANY   -- Branches of foreign banks may not act as banks of deposit for mutual funds of German investment companies. In the interest of investor protection and prudential control the regulations on investment companies require that only legally independent domestic banks -- including subsidiaries of foreign banks -- may be admitted as banks of deposit for the funds and securities of investment companies. The exclusion of foreign branches from this type of business is of no practical relevance to their activities in Germany.

             -- For the management of and participation in domestic security issues as well as issues of foreigners -- in practice denominated in domestic currency only -- there are no legal provisions which would in any way distinguish between domestic banks, including foreign-owned banks established in Germany, and foreign-banks, whether operating from abroad or domiciled domestically in the form of a branch.

             -- However, there is a "gentlemen's agreement" on the issuing of foreign Deutsche Mark bonds which the Deutsche Bundesbank has concluded on a voluntary basis with the most important German banks in the field of issues of foreigners. Inter alia, these banks have agreed to participate in the syndication and selling of foreign Deutsche Mark bonds only under the condition that a domestic bank act as a lead manager. The increasing use of the Deutsche Mark as a denomination currency for international bond issues made it advisable to introduce such arrangements for reasons of monetary and capital market policy.

-- Foreign banks are free to participate in Eurobond syndications as co-manager or ordinary member.

-- Decisions on the overall volume considered feasible under the prevailing market conditions and the order of individual public or private issues are taken by a Sub-Committee for Foreign Deutsche Mark Bonds of the the Central Capital Market Committee. This is a voluntary co-ordinating body which is currently composed of six leading syndicate banks and a representative of the Deutsche Bundesbank as a permanent guest.

GREECE   -- None

IRELAND   -- None

ITALY   -- Branches of foreign banks are allowed to extend individual loans that do not exceed three-fifths of their own funds. Loans in excess of this limit must be authorised by the Bank of Italy. There is no limit set on the excess amounts. This regulation applies to Italian branches of foreign banks whose parents have provided the Bank of Italy with a "comfort letter". In the absence of this, the limit for individual loans is set at two-fifths of the endowment fund.

-- Foreign branches, like domestic banks, can only operate in the short-term area (up to eighteen months). Nevertheless, they may extend credit beyond the short-term within ceilings that vary for each branch from 10 to 15 per cent of their borrowed funds. The percentage applied rises in parallel with the ratio of the branch's own funds to its borrowed funds. In the absence of a "comfort letter", deposits -- rather than borrowed funds -- are taken as the reference parameter for lending operations beyond the short term.

-- Lending by the branches of foreign banks is also restricted territorially as follows:

   i) To the regions in whose provincial capitals the branches are established (without any restriction on the nationality of the borrower);

   ii) To the whole country in the case of lending to firms of foreign origin or subsidiaries of foreign companies.

JAPAN   -- None

LUXEMBOURG   -- None

NETHERLANDS   -- For the management of and participation in security issues, the general attitude of the Dutch authorities is that the management group for syndicated guilder loans should be mainly domestic. More specifically, a domestic bank is supposed to act as lead manager of bond or notes issues and the management group for syndicated loans should include domestic banks as co-managers.

-- Banks, established outside the Netherlands, are allowed to act as co-manager of bond and notes issues; their total underwriting participation (bonds) or their total number (notes) is subject to certain limitations. The same rules as described above with respect to domestic banks, apply to foreign-owned banks established in the Netherlands, unless the nature of their participation warrants a different attitude.

NEW ZEALAND -- Existing commercial banks which are foreign-owned or have foreign participation are subject to the same rules or treatment as indigenous banks. In general terms, the same applies to merchant banks with overseas participation. However, any overseas resident (including companies with more than 25 per cent foreign equity) requires Overseas Investment Commission approval to borrow in New Zealand over a limit of NZ$ 300 000. In practice, this limit is not a constraint on foreign merchant banks as approval is readily forthcoming in normal business cases.

NORWAY -- Not applicable.

PORTUGAL -- The three foreign-owned banks operating in Portugal are subject to the same provisions applying to indigenous banks but they are not allowed to accept deposits or grant credit under the savings-credit system established for Portuguese emigrants in 1976.

SPAIN -- Foreign banks established under the provisions of the Royal Decree 1388/1978 are subject to the following specific restrictions in addition to any regulation applicable to Spanish banks:

i) Except if expressly authorised by the Bank of Spain, outside financing raised on the domestic market may not exceed 40 per cent of total assets. This limitation does not include financing raised on the Spanish interbank market;

ii) Their security portfolio must consist exclusively of Government and private bonds and, exceptionally for no more than six months, of shares purchased in settlement of debts corresponding to loans made in good faith. They may also hold - with the approval of the Ministry of the Economy and subject to authorisations required by foreign investment regulations - up to 100 per cent of the capital of companies operating in the credit-card business, data processing and other auxiliary banking services.

SWEDEN -- Not applicable.

SWITZERLAND -- Foreign-owned banks established in Switzerland are authorised to be lead managers of borrowings in Swiss francs or in foreign currencies. They have the same rights as Swiss banks.

TURKEY -- None.

UNITED
KINGDOM
-- Guidance on the arrangements which the Bank of England England wishes to see observed for new issues in the United Kingdom capital markets is set out in the Bank's notice of 11th November 1980. This states that to enable the impact of new issues on the sterling capital market to be monitored adequately, the Bank wishes to see all capital issues in sterling led by a United Kingdom-based institution with the capacity in the United Kingdom to act as an issuing house. Foreign-owned institutions with such a capacity will be eligible to lead sterling issues if in the Bank's view there are reciprocal opportunities in their domestic capital markets for equivalent United Kingdom-owned institutions; but the Bank will expect such issues to be co-led by a United Kingdom-owned institution with the capacity in the United Kingdom to act as an issuing house. Foreign-owned institutions which do not meet the reciprocity requirement will be eligible to participate in a co-management position but not as a leader or co-leader.

UNITED
STATES
-- Banks' access to state government and other state public authorities' deposits is determined by state authorities.

-- United States bank holding companies may not acquire more than 5 per cent of the shares of a non-financial commercial and industrial enterprise, but foreign banking organisations may, under certain circumstances, acquire equity participations of more than 5 per cent in such enterprises.

Table 3.3

OTHER DIFFERENTIAL RESTRICTIONS AFFECTING
FOREIGN-OWNED BANKS, INCLUDING ADMINISTRATIVE PRACTICES
THAT BEAR MORE HEAVILY UPON FOREIGN BANKS (*)

AUSTRALIA   -- None

AUSTRIA   -- Upon request foreign banks may participate in export financing.

BELGIUM   -- None

CANADA   -- None

DENMARK   -- None

FINLAND   -- There are no legal barriers for foreign-owned banks obtaining
                 discount credit. Central bank credit is extended to a limited
                 number of banks in various tranches which are defined in terms
                 of basic central credit quotas. The quotas are set by
                 assessing the nature and volume of a bank's business as well as
                 its seasonal and cyclical variability. Without historical
                 evidence to assess these factors, assigning a quota to a newly
                 established bank, either domestically or foreign owned, would
                 be difficult and/or arbitrary. It was therefore decided not to
                 assign quotas at least for the time being to foreign-owned
                 banks, the first of which was opened in March 1981. This is
                 not intended to be discriminatory nor is it so in practice:
                 there are larger domestically-owned banks which do not have
                 direct access to central bank credit. Moreover, foreign
                 subsidiaries have been granted access to a check overdraft
                 facility at the central bank.

FRANCE   -- Regulatory provisions apply equally to both domestic and
                 foreign-owned banks. In practice, credit ceilings
                 ("encadrement du crédit") may bear more heavily on
                 recently-established banks and on those banks with an important
                 part of their activity represented by operations in French
                 francs with residents. But these hindrances apply equally to
                 both French banks and foreign-controlled banks. Moreover,
                 these latter banks may be granted by the Banque de France
                 special, temporary derogations to credit ceiling provisions
                 with a view to facilitating their establishment in France.

GERMANY   -- There are no limitations on access by foreign-owned banks to
                 government aids and measures. This is also true with regard to
                 foreign-owned banks' access to official rediscounting
                 facilities on favourable terms through the Ausfuhrkredit GmbH
                 "AKA". (AKA is a private association of German banks founded
                 in order to provide funds for export financing. It is not

---

* This Table summarises answers to items 3.3 to 3.9 of the questionnaire.

government controlled. Its main credit facility, the so-called Plafond A -- and Plafond C as a part of Plafond A -- consists exclusively of funds from the AKA-member banks. It is not accessible to non-member banks. The other export credit facility associated with AKA is the so-called Plafond B. It is a rediscount facility with the Deutsche Bundesbank and is open to all domestic banks including foreign-owned institutions.) However, foreign-owned banks will not normally be granted government guaranties for export credits directed to the country of residence of the parent institutions.

GREECE -- Exchange-control restrictions apply to the repatriation of profits and contributions to head-office overhead expenses:

  i) After-tax profits of foreign banks' branches may be repatriated up to the amount of foreign exchange imported from their offshore operations. Alternatively, the monetary authorities may approve repatriation of profits up to a small percentage of deposits for branches with limited offshore activity;

  ii) Dividends of non-resident shareholders in Greek banks may be repatriated up to 3 per cent (or after special approval 6 per cent) of their imported capital participation;

  iii) Branches of foreign banks may repatriate contributions to head-office overhead expenses up to 1.5 per cent of the gross interest margins of the bank provided that an equal amount of foreign exchange has been imported from offshore operations in excess of the amount necessary to cover repatriation of profits.

IRELAND -- Access to officially-supported arrangements for export credit financing has been historically confined to the four Associated Banks only (two of which are foreign-owned). The extension of the scheme to other banks is under consideration.

ITALY -- None

JAPAN -- None

LUXEMBOURG -- None

NETHERLANDS -- None

NEW ZEALAND -- Existing commercial banks which are foreign-owned or have foreign participation are subject to the same rules or treatment as indigenous banks. However, certain differential tax provisions apply to non-resident merchant banks, with the exact nature of this depending upon the existence of bilateral taxation agreements. Also, all companies are subject to exchange controls on the remittance of interest, profits and dividends. However, it has always been exchange control policy to approve the remittance of interest, profits and dividends earned in New Zealand by non-resident beneficiaries, with only a purely technical proviso that prior approval be sought from the Reserve Bank.

NORWAY   -- Not applicable.

PORTUGAL   -- Rules and regulations apply uniformly to both domestic and foreign-owned banks. The repatriation by foreign banks of profits and capital is always authorised, although in case of serious difficulties in the external payments position, it may be subject to a time schedule.

SPAIN   -- None

SWEDEN   -- Not applicable.

SWITZERLAND   -- None

TURKEY   -- None

UNITED   -- In general, there are no differential monetary policy
KINGDOM   requirements. However, applications by foreign-owned banks wishing their acceptances to become eligible for discount at the Bank of England are judged on the same basis as are those for domestic banks only after it has been established that British banks enjoy reciprocal opportunities in the foreign owners' domestic market.

UNITED   -- None
STATES

Part III

CROSS BORDER INTERNATIONAL BANKING OPERATIONS (*)

AUSTRALIA   -- Resident deposits with foreign-based banks:

    a) Foreign currency:

      -- Residents (bank and non-bank) are permitted to conduct working accounts where continuing commercial need can be demonstrated;

      -- Working balances may be deposited at interest pending use to meet firm foreign currency commitments falling due within one month - where no such commitments exist repatriation is required immediately;

      -- Holding of deposits for investment purposes is not permitted.

    b) Australian currency: residents are generally not permitted to hold Australian currency deposits with foreign-based banks.

-- Authority is generally given for Australian residents to borrow in either foreign or Australian currency provided that the borrowing is on normal commercial terms. However, borrowings by banks for unspecified working capital purposes in Australia are not permitted.

-- Balances in Australian currency accounts with resident banks must be limited to working balances but may include cover for specific approved payments due on a spot basis within one month to Australian residents by non-residents. Balances may not be invested at interest in Australia and may not include counterpart funds of offshore A$ deposits or cover for forward dealings. Non-resident banks may not have foreign currency accounts with resident banks.

-- As a general point, along with other non-residents, foreign-based banks are permitted to invest in equity shares subject to the Government's normal foreign investment guidelines. Residents would generally be permitted to enter into arrangements with foreign-based banks for services provided overseas on the basis that the underlying transactions conform with exchange control requirements. Use by residents of locally issued credit cards is preferred but use overseas of foreign bank credit cards may be authorised where a specific need is established.

---

* This Table summarises answers to items 4 and 5 of the questionnaire.

AUSTRIA
-- Non-bank borrowing and lending operations with non-resident banks require prior approval from the National Bank. No licences are issued to resident non-banks for capital outflows in order to create balances with foreign credit institutions.

-- An individual licence is required for domestic banks placing domestic-currency funds with non-resident banks.

-- External foreign-currency borrowing by domestic banks for relending abroad requires individual authorisation which is issued automatically for credits maturing within one year. The total of such borrowing is subject to a ceiling.

BELGIUM
-- None (but international transactions are affected by the existence of a two-tier foreign-exchange market).

-- The solicitation of public savings in the form of reimbursable funds or placement of securities is forbidden except if it is exercised within the scope of the existing provisions relating to the protection of savings. Thus, any foreign bank without an offshoot in Belgium cannot carry on operations aimed at soliciting public savings.

CANADA
-- None

DENMARK
-- Residents are generally not allowed to hold accounts with non-resident banks (4) except when (i) the funds are held with foreign banks abroad no longer than 30 days or are used in legal transactions with other non-residents (insurance and shipping companies are subject to more liberal rules) or (ii) the accounts are held by Danish banks with correspondents abroad, if the individual bank's net foreign position does not exceed 15 per cent of the bank's net capital, and if the terms of the account do not exceed 7 days notice (in case the account matches deposits from a non-resident or forward transactions the notice applied may correspond to the terms of that of the matching deposit or forward transaction).

-- Residents can raise loans from foreign banks if the loan is raised with a view to financing foreign trade (commercial credit) or business investment and current expenses (financial loan with a maturity of at least five years) or if the loan is raised by Danish banks and the individual bank's net foreign liabilities do not exceed the bank's net foreign assets.

-- Foreign banks can hold accounts with Danish banks if the Danish bank's net foreign liabilities do not exceed its net foreign assets.

-- Foreign banks can carry out portfolio investment in all Danish bonds and shares quoted at the Copenhagen Stock Exchange.

FINLAND
-- Resident banks may hold deposits with non-resident banks in both domestic and foreign currency as long as their foreign exchange positions are covered. Resident non-banks require

permission to hold deposits in domestic and foreign currency with non-resident banks.

-- Resident bank and non-bank borrowing in foreign and domestic currency from non-resident banks is subject to prior approval when it is not used to finance normal export credits and suppliers' credits of up to twelve months.

-- Holdings of current deposits by non-resident banks in domestic and foreign currency with resident banks does not require prior authorisation.

-- Other cross-border capital transactions (except normal export credit and suppliers' credits up to twelve months) by residents involving foreign currency require authorisation.

FRANCE
-- Unless a special derogation is granted, French residents are not allowed to hold deposits at banks domiciled abroad.

-- Residents' borrowing abroad is subject to exchange-control regulations.

-- Lending denominated in French francs to non-residents is usually not permitted.

-- The provision to residents by banks located abroad of other banking services which imply a transfer of funds (e.g. portfolio management, credit cards) is prohibited.

GERMANY
-- None

GREECE
-- Banks conducting business from non-resident offices with residents of Greece are subject to the full range of exchange controls on capital movements. This implies that in the case where the realization of a loan transaction requires repayment in foreign exchange by a resident of Greece, prior monetary authorities' approval is required. Exception: Transactions with shipping firms having receipts in foreign exchange.

IRELAND
-- There is no limit to the amount of foreign-currency deposits which Irish banks (5) may place with foreign-based banks (i.e. lend foreign currency). Banks may not place Irish pound deposits (i.e. lend Irish pounds) with foreign-based banks without the specific approval of the Central Bank.

-- There is no limit to the amount of foreign currency borrowings (i.e. deposits) which Irish banks (4) may have from foreign-based banks. Irish pound borrowings (i.e. deposits) are in general limited to a maximum of £250 000 from any one foreign-based bank.

-- Irish residents (5) are prohibited from holding deposits in either Irish pounds or foreign currency at foreign-based banks unless approved by the Central Bank.

-- Irish residents (5) are prohibited from borrowing either Irish pounds or foreign-currency from foreign-based banks unless approved by the Central Bank.

ITALY

-- Holdings of deposits in lire and foreign currency by resident non-banks and in lire by resident banks with non-resident banks are virtually prohibited. Holdings of deposits by resident banks at non-resident banks in foreign currency with maturities up to one year are freely allowed; deposits above one year are subject to authorisation from the Italian Exchange Office.

-- Borrowing from non-resident banks by resident non-banks is subject to prior authorisation, with a few minor exceptions. Borrowing by resident banks is also subject to prior authorisation; nonetheless, some transactions connected with export trade financing are liberalised.

-- Holdings of deposits (in domestic and foreign currency) by non-resident banks with resident banks are free.

-- As a general rule, foreign investments in Italy by non-resident banks are liberalised; other banking services are not allowed freely.

JAPAN

-- Resident non-bank holdings of deposits with non-resident banks are subject to licence.

-- Non-bank borrowings from non-resident banks are subject to prior notification.

LUXEMBOURG

-- None (but international transactions are affected by the existence of a two-tier foreign-exchange market).

NETHERLANDS

-- Borrowing by non-bank residents from non-resident banks whether in guilders or in foreign currency, is subject to individual exchange control licence by the Netherlands Bank, except for (1) an amount up to Gld 500 000 a year per borrower, and (2) mortgage loans on real estate situated abroad.

-- The inward transfer of capital originating from short-term borrowing abroad (i.e. with a maturity of less than two years) by non-bank residents is restricted for reasons of domestic monetary policy. Longer-term borrowing for domestic use by resident enterprises is generally permitted upon application if the loans meet the following conditions: (1) the average maturity shall be at least two years; (2) the rate of interest is not to be adjusted within periods of two years; (3) advance repayment is precluded; and (4) to the extent that the loan is denominated in guilders, the issue of bearer debt certificates shall not be allowed.

-- Other borrowing by non-bank residents is in general permitted only if the proceeds are employed abroad, either for direct investment or for repayment of licensed foreign loans raised earlier. Short-term foreign bank credit for the financing of

imports is licensed if it is directly connected with specific
import transactions, taking the place of customary supplier's
credit. As a rule, non-bank residents are not allowed to sell
commercial and other receivables owed by residents or unlisted
domestic fixed-interest securities, among which Netherlands
Treasury paper, to non-residents.

-- For reasons of protection of the domestic capital market,
domestic banks need a licence from the Netherlands Bank to
extend guilder loans to non-residents (banks or non-banks) with
a maturity of two years or more, if such loans exceed
Gld 10 million a year to the same foreign borrower. However,
such a licence is normally given upon application.

NEW ZEALAND -- New Zealand's exchange control regulations of 1978
substantially preclude external banks from seeking deposits in
New Zealand from New Zealand residents or companies. Under the
regulations, the acquisition of financial assets overseas,
including bank deposits, involving a remittance from New
Zealand would normally not be permitted. Foreign currency
arising from the proceeds of exports and services rendered must
be sold to a New Zealand trading bank and authorised foreign
exchange dealer. Overseas borrowings by individuals, and by
branches of overseas incorporated companies are covered by the
exchange control regulations of 1978. New Zealand incorporated
companies are additionally covered by the overseas investment
regulations of 1974 but these impose no additional substantive
requirements. Under current policy overseas borrowings (from
banks or other sources) are freely approved provided:

i) The funds are remitted to New Zealand through the banking
system or disbursed offshore for an approved purpose;

ii) The loan is for a specified term of not less than twelve
months and repayments are fixed according to a
pre-determined schedule;

iii) Fees and interest rates are in line with those charged on
similar loans in the market concerned.

-- Importers and exporters do not require consent to raise funds
overseas to finance their foreign trade providing the terms of
the borrowing is less than twelve months.

NORWAY -- Since March 1980 authorised banks have been required to keep
their overall foreign exchange positions (spot plus forward) in
approximate balance on a daily basis. The permissible margins
are commensurate with the banks' total assets. Holdings of
foreign currency deposits by resident banks with foreign-based
banks do not require any prior approval from Norges Bank.
Holdings of kroner deposits by resident banks with foreign
based banks will not be accepted. Business enterprises which
have both income and expenditures in foreign currency are
allowed to open foreign currency accounts with foreign banks.
The notice of withdrawal for deposits on such accounts shall

not exceed 30 days unless Norges Bank has granted special permission. In addition, companies which have extensive business operations abroad and long-term commitments in foreign currency are, on application, allowed to hedge against exchange rate risks by placing parts of their foreign exchange holdings as bank deposits and/or in quoted foreign bonds of whatever maturity. Licences for the purchase of foreign bonds are restricted to those currencies in which the applicant has long-term debts. Holdings of kroner deposits by non-bank residents with foreign-based banks will not be accepted. The general public is not allowed to open foreign currency accounts with foreign banks.

-- Foreign currency borrowing from foreign-based banks by resident banks does not require individual authorisation. Issues of kroner or foreign currency bond loans abroad are subject to prior approval from the Ministry of Finance. Permission from Norges Bank is required for resident non-banks receiving loans from foreign-based banks. The total foreign exchange borrowing is subject to a ceiling. Permission to raise bank loans abroad denominated in Norwegian kroner is at present rarely granted.

-- With regard to non-residents' accounts with Norwegian banks -- whether in Norwegian kroner or in foreign currency -- the authorised banks have been given general permission to establish such accounts without Norges Bank's prior consent. At present there is no ceiling on the balances on such accounts.

-- Non-residents, including foreign-based banks, are permitted to make portfolio investments in listed Norwegian shares without any licence from Norges Bank. This also refers to units in listed Norwegian unit trusts specializing in shares. Shares and units may be sold to non-residents within the limits stipulated in other legislation and/or in the articles of association of the companies concerned. On application, listed Norwegian bearer bonds can be sold to non-residents within a ceiling of maximum 1 million kroner per investor.

-- Credit cards issued by a Norwegian subsidiary of a non-resident company can be used without prior consent from Norges Bank. If credit cards are issued by a non-resident company, a licence is required.

PORTUGAL -- Direct foreign-exchange operations are not allowed for the non-banking sector. Indeed, every foreign-exchange operation shall have to be effected by the "intermédiaires agrées"; these are subject, such as any other resident, to the exchange control regulations in force as regards the operations which they carry out for their own account. Non-bank residents may hold foreign currency only for very short periods, after which it will have to be surrendered to credit institutions authorised to deal in foreign exchange.

-- The opening of demand or time deposit accounts in escudos, in the name of non-residents (banks and non-banking sector) is subject to authorisation. Debiting and crediting of such accounts, usually called "foreign accounts in escudos", are subject to some conditions. Loans under the form of overdrafts require prior authorisation from the Banco de Portugal; as to accounts opened in the name of correspondents abroad "mail overdrafts" are allowed for a period not above 8 days.

-- The opening in Portugal of accounts in foreign currency (demand, notice and time deposits) in the name both of residents and non-residents is subject to the general principle of authorisation.

-- Non-bank residents are not allowed to open deposit accounts abroad; the opening of such accounts may be authorised only on an exceptional basis in the case of some enterprises (public-sector enterprises, insurance companies, etc.) when justified by their external operations. The Banco de Portugal establishes the principles governing the debiting and crediting of foreign-exchange accounts opened by domestic credit institutions with banks abroad.

SPAIN
-- Resident non-banks' foreign-currency operations with non-resident banks require individual authorisation. Resident non-banks' holdings of domestic-currency deposits with non-resident banks are forbidden.

-- Spanish resident banks are subject to exchange control regulations insofar as operations on their own account are concerned. However "authorised" banks are free to accept foreign-currency deposits from non-resident banks provided that the proceeds are on-lent abroad, to other resident banks or to previously authorised non-bank residents. Foreign-currency borrowing through any instrument other than deposits is subject to authorisation.

SWEDEN
-- Payments to and from Sweden shall be transferred through those Swedish banks that are authorised to trade in foreign currency and examined in accordance with the Swedish Exchange Control Regulations.

-- Swedish borrowing abroad requires authorisation from the Riksbank. Except for a few specified categories of borrowing, such authorisation is at present normally granted. Lending to non-residents, with the exception of commercial credits, is generally not permitted. Authorised banks are allowed to extend credits of not more than six months' maturity to foreign banks for the financing of Swedish exports. Resident non-banks' accounts with non-resident banks are subject to individual licences with certain exceptions.

SWITZERLAND -- No restrictions concerning capital movements or foreign-exchange transactions.

-- Banks not domiciled in Switzerland are not allowed to participate in syndicates for the issue on the Swiss market of securities denominated in Swiss francs.

TURKEY
-- Turkish residents (non-banks) are allowed to hold deposits at foreign-based banks within the framework of foreign exchange regulations.

-- Foreign-based banks can open credits to Turkish residents through an intermediary resident-bank approved by the Undersecretariat of Treasury and Foreign Trade.

UNITED KINGDOM
-- None

UNITED STATES
-- None

NOTES AND REFERENCES

1. Two foreign banks -- the Bank of New Zealand (BNZ) and the Banque
    Nationale de Paris (BNP), which have both been represented in Australia
    since last century -- currently hold trading (i.e. commercial) bank
    authorities. The Bank of New Zealand Savings Bank (BNZSB), a
    wholly-owned subsidiary of BNZ, was granted authority in 1972 to carry
    on savings bank business in Australia.

2. The issue of foreign bank entry has been under consideration by the
    Government since 1981. In the spring of 1983 the Government decided to
    appoint a new committee to study the credit market structure that had
    developed in recent years. Against this background the committee
    should study the question of establishment of foreign banks as well as
    of foreign finance companies.

3. See also the United Kingdom entry in Table 2.1.

4. According to the Danish foreign exchange regulations, foreign
    subsidiaries and branches abroad of Danish banks are regarded as
    non-resident institutions. Foreign banks operating in Denmark through
    a branch are regarded as residents as far as branch business is
    concerned.

5. "Irish banks" refer only to those banks authorised to deal in foreign
    exchange.

6. "Irish residents" refer to all Irish non-bank residents and those banks
    not authorised to deal in foreign exchange.

OECD SALES AGENTS
DÉPOSITAIRES DES PUBLICATIONS DE L'OCDE

ARGENTINA – ARGENTINE
Carlos Hirsch S.R.L., Florida 165, 4° Piso (Galería Guemes)
1333 BUENOS AIRES, Tel. 33.1787.2391 y 30.7122

AUSTRALIA – AUSTRALIE
Australia and New Zealand Book Company Pty., Ltd.,
10 Aquatic Drive, Frenchs Forest, N.S.W. 2086
P.O. Box 459, BROOKVALE, N.S.W. 2100

AUSTRIA – AUTRICHE
OECD Publications and Information Center
4 Simrockstrasse 5300 Bonn (Germany). Tel. (0228) 21.60.45
Local Agent/Agent local :
Gerold and Co., Graben 31, WIEN 1. Tel. 52.22.35

BELGIUM – BELGIQUE
Jean De Lannoy, Service Publications OCDE
avenue du Roi 202, B-1060 BRUXELLES. Tel. 02/538.51.69

BRAZIL – BRÉSIL
Mestre Jou S.A., Rua Guaipa 518,
Caixa Postal 24090, 05089 SAO PAULO 10. Tel. 261.1920
Rua Senador Dantas 19 s/205-6, RIO DE JANEIRO GB.
Tel. 232.07.32

CANADA
Renouf Publishing Company Limited,
2182 ouest, rue Ste-Catherine,
MONTRÉAL, Qué. H3H 1M7. Tel. (514)937.3519
OTTAWA, Ont. K1P 5A6, 61 Sparks Street

DENMARK – DANEMARK
Munksgaard Export and Subscription Service
35, Nørre Søgade
DK 1370 KØBENHAVN K. Tel. +45.1.12.85.70

FINLAND – FINLANDE
Akateeminen Kirjakauppa
Keskuskatu 1, 00100 HELSINKI 10. Tel. 65.11.22

FRANCE
Bureau des Publications de l'OCDE,
2 rue André-Pascal, 75775 PARIS CEDEX 16. Tel. (1) 524.81.67
Principal correspondant :
13602 AIX-EN-PROVENCE : Librairie de l'Université.
Tel. 26.18.08

GERMANY – ALLEMAGNE
OECD Publications and Information Center
4 Simrockstrasse 5300 BONN Tel. (0228) 21.60.45

GREECE – GRÈCE
Librairie Kauffmann, 28 rue du Stade,
ATHÈNES 132. Tel. 322.21.60

HONG-KONG
Government Information Services,
Publications/Sales Section, Baskerville House,
2nd Floor. 22 Ice House Street

ICELAND – ISLANDE
Snaebjörn Jónsson and Co., h.f.,
Hafnarstraeti 4 and 9, P.O.B. 1131, REYKJAVIK.
Tel. 13133/14281/11936

INDIA – INDE
Oxford Book and Stationery Co. :
NEW DELHI-1, Scindia House. Tel. 45896
CALCUTTA 700016, 17 Park Street. Tel. 240832

INDONESIA – INDONÉSIE
PDIN-LIPI, P.O. Box 3065/JKT., JAKARTA, Tel. 583467

IRELAND – IRLANDE
TDC Publishers – Library Suppliers
12 North Frederick Street, DUBLIN 1 Tel. 744835-749677

ITALY – ITALIE
Libreria Commissionaria Sansoni :
Via Lamarmora 45, 50121 FIRENZE. Tel. 579751/584468
Via Bartolini 29, 20155 MILANO. Tel. 365083
Sub-depositari :
Ugo Tassi
Via A. Farnese 28, 00192 ROMA. Tel. 310590
Editrice e Libreria Herder,
Piazza Montecitorio 120, 00186 ROMA. Tel. 6794628
Costantino Ercolano, Via Generale Orsini 46, 80132 NAPOLI. Tel. 405210
Libreria Hoepli, Via Hoepli 5, 20121 MILANO. Tel. 865446
Libreria Scientifica, Dott. Lucio de Biasio "Aeiou"
Via Meravigli 16, 20123 MILANO Tel. 807679
Libreria Zanichelli
Piazza Galvani 1/A, 40124 Bologna Tel. 237389
Libreria Lattes, Via Garibaldi 3, 10122 TORINO. Tel. 519274
La diffusione delle edizioni OCSE è inoltre assicurata dalle migliori librerie nelle
città più importanti.

JAPAN – JAPON
OECD Publications and Information Center,
Landic Akasaka Bldg., 2-3-4 Akasaka,
Minato-ku, TOKYO 107 Tel. 586.2016

KOREA – CORÉE
Pan Korea Book Corporation,
P.O. Box n° 101 Kwangwhamun, SÉOUL. Tel. 72.7369

LEBANON – LIBAN
Documenta Scientifica/Redico,
Edison Building, Bliss Street, P.O. Box 5641, BEIRUT.
Tel. 354429 – 344425

MALAYSIA – MALAISIE
University of Malaya Co-operative Bookshop Ltd.
P.O. Box 1127, Jalan Pantai Baru
KUALA LUMPUR. Tel. 51425, 54058, 54361

THE NETHERLANDS – PAYS-BAS
Staatsuitgeverij, Verzendboekhandel,
Chr. Plantijnstraat 1 Postbus 20014
2500 EA S-GRAVENHAGE. Tel. nr. 070.789911
Voor bestellingen: Tel. 070.789208

NEW ZEALAND – NOUVELLE-ZÉLANDE
Publications Section,
Government Printing Office Bookshops:
AUCKLAND: Retail Bookshop: 25 Rutland Street,
Mail Orders: 85 Beach Road, Private Bag C.P.O.
HAMILTON: Retail: Ward Street,
Mail Orders, P.O. Box 857
WELLINGTON: Retail: Mulgrave Street (Head Office),
Cubacade World Trade Centre
Mail Orders: Private Bag
CHRISTCHURCH: Retail: 159 Hereford Street,
Mail Orders: Private Bag
DUNEDIN: Retail: Princes Street
Mail Order: P.O. Box 1104

NORWAY – NORVÈGE
J.G. TANUM A/S
P.O. Box 1177 Sentrum OSLO 1. Tel. (02) 80.12.60

PAKISTAN
Mirza Book Agency, 65 Shahrah Quaid-E-Azam, LAHORE 3.
Tel. 66839

PHILIPPINES
National Book Store, Inc.
Library Services Division, P.O. Box 1934, MANILA.
Tel. Nos. 49.43.06 to 09, 40.53.45, 49.45.12

PORTUGAL
Livraria Portugal, Rua do Carmo 70-74,
1117 LISBOA CODEX. Tel. 360582/3

SINGAPORE – SINGAPOUR
Information Publications Pte Ltd,
Pei-Fu Industrial Building,
24 New Industrial Road N° 02-06
SINGAPORE 1953, Tel. 2831786, 2831798

SPAIN – ESPAGNE
Mundi-Prensa Libros, S.A.
Castelló 37, Apartado 1223, MADRID-1. Tel. 275.46.55
Libreria Bosch, Ronda Universidad 11, BARCELONA 7.
Tel. 317.53.08, 317.53.58

SWEDEN – SUÈDE
AB CE Fritzes Kungl Hovbokhandel,
Box 16 356, S 103 27 STH, Regeringsgatan 12,
DS STOCKHOLM. Tel. 08/23.89.00
Subscription Agency/Abonnements :
Wennergren-Williams AB,
Box 13004, S104 25 STOCKHOLM.
Tel. 08/54.12.00

SWITZERLAND – SUISSE
OECD Publications and Information Center
4 Simrockstrasse 5300 BONN (Germany). Tel. (0228) 21.60.45
Local Agents/Agents locaux
Librairie Payot, 6 rue Grenus, 1211 GENÈVE 11. Tel. 022.31.89.50

TAIWAN – FORMOSE
Good Faith Worldwide Int'l Co., Ltd.
9th floor, No. 118, Sec. 2,
Chung Hsiao E. Road
TAIPEI. Tel. 391.7396/391.7397

THAILAND – THAILANDE
Suksit Siam Co., Ltd., 1715 Rama IV Rd,
Samyan, BANGKOK 5. Tel. 2511630

TURKEY – TURQUIE
Kültur Yayinlari Is-Türk Ltd. Sti.
Atatürk Bulvari No : 191/Kat. 21
Kavaklidere/ANKARA. Tel. 17 02 66
Dolmabahce Cad. No : 29
BESIKTAS/ISTANBUL. Tel. 60 71 88

UNITED KINGDOM – ROYAUME-UNI
H.M. Stationery Office.
P.O.B. 276, LONDON SW8 5DT.
(postal orders only)
Telephone orders: (01) 622.3316, or
49 High Holborn, LONDON WC1V 6 HB (personal callers)
Branches at: EDINBURGH, BIRMINGHAM, BRISTOL,
MANCHESTER, BELFAST.

UNITED STATES OF AMERICA – ÉTATS-UNIS
OECD Publications and Information Center, Suite 1207,
1750 Pennsylvania Ave., N.W. WASHINGTON, D.C.20006 – 4582
Tel. (202) 724.1857

VENEZUELA
Libreria del Este, Avda. F. Miranda 52, Edificio Galipan,
CARACAS 106. Tel. 32.23.01/33.26.04/31.58.38

YUGOSLAVIA – YOUGOSLAVIE
Jugoslovenska Knjiga, Knez Mihajlova 2, P.O.B. 36, BEOGRAD.
Tel. 621.992

Les commandes provenant de pays où l'OCDE n'a pas encore désigné de dépositaire peuvent être adressées à :
OCDE, Bureau des Publications, 2, rue André-Pascal, 75775 PARIS CEDEX 16.
Orders and inquiries from countries where sales agents have not yet been appointed may be sent to:
OECD, Publications Office, 2, rue André-Pascal, 75775 PARIS CEDEX 16.

67587-05-1984

OECD PUBLICATIONS, 2, rue André-Pascal, 75775 PARIS CEDEX 16 - No. 42913 1984
PRINTED IN FRANCE
(21 84 03 1) ISBN 92-64-12586-8